A DOCTOR OF SORTS

A DOCTOR
OF SORTS

In Peace and In War

by
V.J. DOWNIE

LEO COOPER

LONDON

First published in Great Britain in 1992 by
LEO COOPER
190 Shaftesbury Avenue, London WC2H 8JL
an imprint of
Pen & Sword Books Ltd.,
47 Church Street, Barnsley, S. Yorks S70 2AS

ISBN 085052 351 6

A CIP catalogue record for this book is available
from the British Library

Typeset by Yorkshire Web, Barnsley, South Yorkshire
in Plantin Roman 10½ point

Printed in Great Britain by
Redwood Press
Melksham, Wiltshire

CONTENTS

To my friends, dead or alive

My thanks are due to Sue Bradbury, of the Folio Society, for her invaluable advice and help in the preparation of this little book, and to Leo Cooper, Tom Hartman and Beryl Hill for their patience and kindness while shepherding it into the light of day.

Prologue

Kamal, the old gardener, was pruning the Sultan's roses when he looked up to see the figure of Death in a corner of the garden. The figure raised its hand and seemed to beckon. Kamal rushed into the palace.

'O Great Master!' he cried to the Sultan, 'I have just seen the figure of Death, and he beckoned to me. I beg you, lend me a horse so that I may flee to Damascus.'

The Sultan was none too pleased, but good gardeners were hard to come by and he didn't want to lose Kamal.

'All right,' he said, 'You can borrow the old grey mare, but be back by Monday, and,' he added, 'don't expect any wages while you are away.'

An hour or so later, when the sun was going down, the Sultan was strolling in the garden and he too saw the figure of Death.

'Hey, you!' he called. He had seen a lot of Death in his time, and he couldn't stand the chap. 'What the devil do you mean by coming into my garden and beckoning to my gardener? You've scared him out of his wits.'

'You do me an injustice, noble Sultan,' said Death. 'I did not beckon to Kamal; I merely raised my hand in a gesture of surprise to see him still working in your garden ... because I have an appointment with him in Damascus tonight.'

A likely tale, you may think, but I have a fellow feeling for the Sultan, for I too have seen a great deal of death − and like the Sultan I hate it. I hate the sight, the smell, and at times the fearsome sound of it. There is, too, a moral in the story: one cannot flee from death but only regret that it is ordained without regard to justice, merit or compassion. In the Sultan's day there was little that he could have done to help poor old Kamal, but times have changed. There are new sophisticated weapons in our armoury, and while Death will always claim the final victory it is no longer a walkover.

This book is concerned with the eternal conflict between life and death, but it makes no pretensions to erudition or instruction in the art of healing. It is only a miscellany of reminiscences set down in random fashion, because memories do not come in chronological or orderly sequence but as wayward thoughts which coalesce to form a picture of the whole. My narrative is in three parts; the first 'Medicine', being mostly about doctors and patients. The second, 'War', is about the one we had between 1939 and 1945. For most of that time I was employed in Field Ambulances: very little has been written about these units, in which the senior medical officers were less concerned with the practice of medicine than with the practices of soldiers; ours and those of the other side. During the war I managed to forget everything I had learned so laboriously about the craft of surgery and in 1945 I had to start again from the beginning. In the third part I have ventured some reflections on two aspects of the human condition which touch us all from time to time.

The accounts of incidents which concern my patients and my companions are true to the best of my recollection, but many of the characters are long since dead and I have tried to ensure that none of them, except those whose names are mentioned in full, could be recognized by others.

PART ONE

MEDICINE

A sidelong look at some aspects of the healing art

Felo De Se

Felo de se sounds much more elegant than suicide, and literally means 'felon of himself'. Perhaps it is an antecedent of that modern snippet of home-spun philosophy ... ''e's a fool to 'isself.'

He was dead. I could see that. His throat was cut, more or less from ear to ear.

I had qualified as a doctor two days before and this was my first patient. Why, I thought miserably, did he have to be dead? I had lain awake in my little room in the doctors' quarters waiting for the call which I knew must come that night. The whole hospital, a huge teaching hospital, depended on me: I was sure of it. My room was small and dingy, with an old wardrobe, a chair and an iron bedstead. In those days we did not have the luxury of a bedside telephone, and when the Night Sister knocked on the door to tell me I was wanted in Casualty I ran all the way. It was a long way, and I was out of breath.

I stood looking down at my first patient. He was middle-aged and had a big bushy moustache. In my six years as a medical student nobody had ever told me what to do with a dead man. We had been told − at great length − how to try and stop people getting dead but we had never ventured over the threshold of eternity.

The Casualty Porter, a grey-haired old fellow, was all too familiar with the inadequacies and shortcomings of newly-qualified doctors, but he was a nice chap and he came to my rescue.

'Shall I take 'im to the mortuary, sir?'

I gave the old fellow a grateful glance and the man was wheeled away on a trolley. I sat down and lit a cigarette, feeling that I had made a rather undistinguished beginning to my medical career. It was soon to become clear that my debut was even more inauspicious than I had thought. The Resident Surgical Officer, a man regarded by the likes of me as closely related to God, arrived in Casualty.

'Have you seen Ferdy?' he asked. Ferdy was one of the senior hospital consultants.

'No,' I said, 'not for weeks.'

'That's odd,' the R.S.O. went on. 'His wife has just telephoned to say he's cut his throat.'

I looked at the Casualty Porter; he looked at me, and we both looked at the R.S.O.

'My God!' I said, and the three of us ran to the mortuary. That, too, was a long way away and we were all out of breath as we looked at the body. It was still on its trolley and it *was* Ferdy. It's astonishing what a difference a cut throat makes to a chap's appearance.

Since that night I have seen scores of suicides and attempted suicides, some impulsive and demonstrative, even spurious, others carefully planned and coldly efficient. The emotions which trigger this desperate act, whether unrequited love, despair or impending disgrace, have probably remained constant over the centuries – but the methods by which the felon can choose to assault his or her person are very dependent on circumstance and period. The twentieth century in particular has been a time of change, when the *modi operandi* have altered in line with contemporary technology.

In my young days throat-cutting was a very popular way of escaping from it all. It is out of fashion now, because gentlemen no longer shave with the aptly named cut-throat razor and, rather surprisingly, a certain expertise is required to bring the enterprise to a fatal conclusion. Satisfaction cannot be guaranteed and although someone, somewhere, may have written a treatise on 'Hints for Beginners' I have no intention of giving away the tricks of the trade. Poor Ferdy knew them only too well.

When Mr King C. Gillette brought employment to his native state of Wisconsin by inventing the safety razor he probably had no idea that he was reducing the work load of casualty surgeons worldwide and causing a deal of frustration among potential 'felons of themselves'. Authors of textbooks on forensic medicine and innumerable writers of detective fiction have gone to great lengths in describing just how a suicidally cut throat can be distinguished from that cut by (say) a cuckolded husband or a prospective legatee. All their work has gone to nought. We don't get cut throats any more. Even if there is a decent old-fashioned razor in the house it's never handy when it's wanted. Probably in an attic with grandpa's golf clubs and his shooting stick.

Mr Gillette was not the only innovator with whom would-be suicides had to contend. Their repertoire was further reduced by the chap who thought of getting gas out of the North Sea. From their point of view the trouble with North Sea gas is that it is not poisonous, and at a stroke it abolished the once popular gambit of putting one's head in the gas oven. That old-fashioned stuff, coal gas, contained carbon monoxide – a very nasty gas indeed. It turned its victims pink, which didn't really matter, but it also deprived them of the power of movement (and thus the option of changing their minds) before they lost consciousness – so we will never know how many people who put their heads in gas ovens came to the ultimate decision that their penultimate decision had been an awful mistake.

From the razor in the bathroom and the oven in the kitchen it is a short step to the lavatory, and here in days gone by there was a diabolical instrument to hand for those who thought themselves tired of life. The standard fluid for killing all the household germs known at that time was lysol, and a bottle of this infernal liquid was often to be found beside the lavatory pan. Aspiring candidates for the hereafter were apt to swallow the stuff, with the most dire and ghastly results. At the hospital where I began, and where poor Ferdy ended, the senior waitress in the resident doctors' Mess was called Gladys and was a living tribute to one of England's greatest surgeons. She had swallowed lysol, and he had replaced her gullet with a tube of skin reaching from her throat to her stomach, one of the first operations of its kind ever carried out.

It was perhaps fitting that Gladys devoted the rest of her life to making sure that an endless succession of young doctors had plenty to eat. The word 'plenty' should perhaps be qualified. There were about forty doctors in the Mess and for breakfast we always had bacon, but, years before, some Machiavellian administrator had decreed that only thirty eggs could be fried each morning. I think it was this piece of low cunning that converted a lot of us to the habit of early rising: it was the only way to get an egg. There was one exception to this otherwise inflexible rule: the R.S.O., the demi-god, had bacon *and* an egg whatever time he appeared for breakfast. Perhaps this was because of the difference in our respective work loads. We were up most nights, whereas he was up every night. He was a Fellow of the Royal College of Surgeons, about 32 years old, and a very capable surgeon. His seniority, skill and experience were rewarded in financial as well as gastronomic terms. We were paid twenty-eight shillings a week, while he was paid nearly four pounds. He had the added dignity and status of an office, and I remember being summoned there to explain why I had left the hospital for a couple of hours without permission. Off duty was not a right, but a privilege to be negotiated with one's colleagues and superiors. However, there was no real difficulty about arranging an occasional evening off, and our usual haunt was the grill-room of a local hotel where for five shillings (25p) we had steak and chips, a pint of beer or shandy, coffee and a glass of Drambuie.

We considered ourselves well paid in comparison with our London colleagues, who got no wages at all, and I never heard anyone complain about the hours on duty. The Hospital was our home and we were very content with our lot. The rates of pay and the work load had not changed over many years and we saw no reason why they should ever change. We knew that by dint of hard work we could make our way up the professional ladder to a position on the staff of a hospital, or could save enough money over the years to buy a place in general practice. Until we had achieved such relative affluence there was of course no question of marriage. Times have changed. The resident doctors of today complain interminably about the difficulties of buying a house and supporting their families, and they look forward eagerly to the annual pay round with its automatic increase in basic and overtime rates.

Times have changed too for potential suicides. The unseemly antics in kitchens, bathrooms and lavatories have been superseded by the ubiquitous overdose of sleeping pills, taken comfortably in bed. This has become such a popular way of trying to shuffle off this mortal coil that doctors are very reluctant to prescribe the more dangerous types of pill. What then, frustrated at every turn, is the poor would-be suicide to do? He can of course take a second opinion from the Euthanasia Society ... and some original thinkers devise methods peculiarly their own. I had one patient, temporarily bent on self-destruction, who ate a pound or so of Ronuk furniture polish. I cannot recommend this; it has nothing to offer either to the epicure or the felon. It doesn't work.

In 1940, when I was medical officer to a cavalry school, a sergeant in the nearby ordnance depot decided for some reason which must have seemed right at the time, to shoot himself through the heart. He took his Lee-Enfield rifle, rested the butt on the end of his bed, applied the muzzle to his chest and pulled the trigger. There was a loud bang, but after a pause for reflection he realized that he was still earth-bound and in comparatively good health. However, he was a stolid and determined character so he re-loaded and tried again. Another loud bang, and this time he began to feel a bit out of sorts so he decided on a second opinion ... mine. I found a single entrance hole over his heart and a horrific exit wound at the back of his chest. After quite a short consultation we agreed that he was a hospital case and off he went in the ambulance. The explanation of this apparent miracle was intriguing. When he had reached forward to get at the trigger his body had rotated slightly so that the bullets, instead of entering at right angles, skidded round his ribs and out through the skin at the back of his chest. It looked very much worse than it really was and he made a rapid recovery − a recovery which so far as I know he never regretted.

I am sorry to end this recital of misplaced human endeavour on a sad note. I remember a husband and wife, both about eighty years old, who decided that enough was enough. They would end sixty happy years of marriage as they had begun ... together. Perhaps they had read of Roman aristocrats who cut their wrists and relaxed in a warm bath surrounded by their family and friends, binding up their wounds when the company pleased them and bleeding contentedly into the bath when the conversation showed signs of flagging.

My old Darby and Joan had made a bit of a muddle of things.

The wounds on their wrists were tentative − not enough to do any real harm, but serious enough to warrant their admission to hospital. The sadness stems from the quaint fashion in those days, of sending women to female wards and men to male wards. Nowadays, of course, they would have mucked in together in a unisex ward and the old lady could have savoured the daily uncertainty of wondering whether her bedpan would be brought by a female nurse or a male nurse. The unisex revolution in hospitals started in the Intensive Care Units − on the premise that the patients were so jolly ill that they were unlikely to care about, or even notice, the sex of their neighbours. Even so, there could be disconcerting moments − as when an elderly titled lady was admitted to our I.C.U. after her Rolls Royce was involved in a rather unpleasant accident. On recovering consciousness she was startled to find a man in the next bed − and even more startled when he said, 'Good morning, Milady'. The old girl had never seen her chauffeur out of uniform, and it was a moment before she accepted that this really was the faithful Johnson in the next bed. As neither of these two patients ever commented to us on the propinquity of the other, one can only guess at their feelings. The old aristocrat may not have minded the faithful Johnson's hairy right leg suspended from pulleys in front of her very eyes and emerging as it did from an uncertain jumble of clothes in the vicinity of his crotch ... but one's heart goes out to poor Johnson, who must have suffered the agonies of the damned in his efforts to avoid breaking wind in the presence of his mistress.

Curriculum Vitae

I had to include this chapter to render more intelligible the rest of my narrative ... which has a bad habit of jumping about from place to place, both geographically and chronologically.

I always knew that I would become a doctor — not because of any deep-rooted urge to heal the sick but because my father said so. As a young impecunious Scot he had taken ship to the Far East with the avowed intent of making his fortune — an ambition which he signally failed to achieve. He spent some time in what was then called the colony of Singapore and in Malaya, but he lived for many years in Siam — and our home was littered with elegant mementoes of that country, including a beautifully fashioned silver tray which was a gift from the king; not the King Mongkut who was so unkindly and inaccurately portrayed in the musical *The King and I*, but his son and successor, King Chulalongkorn. I am afraid that my dear old papa was a very poor businessman, and after thirty years he returned to his native Scotland, saddened but not appreciably wiser. He had, however, acquired a beautiful wife and they soon migrated south, ever hopeful of commercial success, to the land of the Sassenach — to the industrial midlands. In his spare time the old boy fathered three sons: one in Bangkok, one in Edinburgh and me, a good deal later on, in Birmingham. He treated the three of us with fine impartiality: he gave us, no doubt in collusion with our mother, rather eccentric Christian names; he sent us, one after the other, to the same school and he made us all into doctors.

The school was King Edward's School, an imposing and smoke-begrimed stone pile slap in the middle of the city of Birmingham. It looked rather like a scaled-down version of the Houses of Parliament, no doubt because the same architect, Sir

Charles Barry, designed both institutions. Perhaps it was this environment which persuaded one of my fellow pupils, Enoch Powell, to make a career in politics. When I knew him he was a quiet boy on the Classics side who gave no hint of the impact he was to make on the nation's affairs. The headmaster, Dr Robert Cary Gilson, who had presided over the school's affairs for a quarter of a century, was a revered and charismatic figure. Tall, bearded, gowned and wearing his mortar board, he swept through the corridors of power like a divine wind, and when we assembled each morning in Big School for daily prayers he would be at his great canopied desk, which had the apposite inscription *Sapientia* carved deeply into the ancient oak above his head. From there he would read the roll call in sonorous tones. Surnames preceded our initials; I was Downie V.J., Enoch was Powell (pronounced Po-el by the Head) J.E., and there was a chap called Blood E.L., whose name we awaited with quiet enjoyment and who went on, I believe, to become a dignitary of the Church. The School was rather good at producing church dignitaries and even managed one Archbishop of Canterbury.

The masters were mostly ex-soldiers from the First World War, captains and majors who maintained discipline with a casual assurance born of long habit in sterner surroundings. Nearly all of them had engaging eccentricities, doubtless contrived to impress their personalities on the boys. Captain Power allowed talking in class unless and until he planted a red flag on his desk with the curt announcement: 'Dangerous to talk now'. After that the merest whisper met with instant retribution. He used a gym shoe instead of a cane but we were required to put our heads under his desk while the punishment was administered. As each blow fell the victim gave an involuntary jerk which banged the back of his head on the underside of the desk. The gallant captain was so well liked that we admired rather than resented this devilish ingenuity.

Captain Street, a tall thin man who was supposed to teach us French, always stood with his back to the classroom fire and his legs spread wide apart. When he wanted to sneeze, which was fairly often, he would bend double so that he was looking backwards between his legs. The sneeze was preceded by a huge intake of breath and the final explosion, accompanied by a loud cry, always sent a shower of sparks and flaming embers on to the hearth. I think these paroxysms were mainly for our entertainment because he never bothered to do it when the fire was out. I can't remember Captain Street ever caning anybody but he had fostered a myth that if he did cane you he'd half kill you. The ploy worked and no one was brave enough to prove the myth unfounded. It was a point of honour not to move or cry out when being caned and I found it hellish painful. I can't remember all my misdemeanours but I was caned twice for smoking, once for saying that the climate of England was equatorial and once for asking the Divinity master, the Revd William Sneath, the meaning of the word 'harlot'. Asking this question was a bit of a dare, and his response was always the same: 'A bad woman, boy, and come out here'. We got three of the best from him and a commendation from our fellows. I expect that the Reverend could reconcile his vigorous correction of impiety with his Christian principles and if he had thought for one moment that the enquiry was based on a genuine thirst for knowledge he might have been more charitable. One can hope, too, that his personal experience of harlots was limited.

Cary Gilson seldom used the cane but punished wrongdoing by the imposition of 'lines', the offender being required to write out a hundred times on specially ruled paper that 'Punctuality is the soul of business'. I must have written that rather smug dictum over a thousand times and it has entered into *my* soul. I am never late for an appointment and all my adult life I have been grateful for the wisdom and the cunning of that redoubtable man. It is far and away the most useful thing I learned at school.

Caning by the masters was accepted as a sorry but inescapable fact of school life. If you broke the rules or failed to maintain acceptable standards of decorum and scholarly application you were caned, or given lines or sentenced to detention — which meant extra work in solitary confinement after school hours. All these punishments were disliked, but a caning by the prefects was something else: it was a much rarer event and was absolutely dreaded. The prefects had authority to cane at the discretion and under the supervision of the head boy, known in our school as the School Captain. He was concerned only with offences such as sneaking or bullying, committed by boys against other boys, and if he authorized a caning the punishment was carried out in the Prefects' Common Room adjoining Big School. Big School itself was a huge vaulted assembly room of church-like dimensions and appearance with an organ at one end and facilities for erecting a stage at the other. It was the heart, and perhaps the soul, of the venerable old building.

One did not have to look far to understand the difference between a punishment meted out by the masters and one inflicted by a prefect. Masters, over the years, developed a grudging affection for their charges and with any luck they might be enfeebled by temporary infirmity or by what we regarded as old age. The boy they were about to cane had not offended against them but against the educational tenets of the time. The prefects, on the other hand, were boys: senior boys, maybe, but not mature enough for compassion to have become part of their nature. Their impending manhood was evidenced only by their burgeoning physique and an athletic prowess which they were eager to demonstrate. Their victim had offended against one of their own and the punishment was vengeful and intended to be both exemplary and memorable. It was certainly a deterrent and, unlike a master's caning, it was held to be a disgrace.

Captain Kirby, the geography master, was called the Pink'un because of his florid complexion and choleric disposition. He was wont to illustrate the relative position and size of the sun and the moon by saying, 'Let us suppose that we have an orange in Big School and a pea in the quadrangle.' The fiery little captain knew that the boys would transpose 'pea' into 'pee' and he would scowl with mock fury at the lewd sniggers which always followed this sally.

Adjoining the quadrangle was a cloistered area which was the venue for three activities not always compatible with each other. The school shooting team, practising for the annual competition at Bisley, used the Cloisters as a rifle range. The targets were at one end and the shooters at the other. In between were two doorways with steps leading down respectively to the washroom and to what was euphemistically called 'the bog'. There was no warning notice as it was felt that any boy wishing to wash his hands or relieve himself should be aware that his need carried with it the risk (admittedly remote) of premature demise. Visitors to the bog were made aware of a little-known geographical fact — that the great city of Birmingham stands upon the River Rea, because the bog was a row of privies set above a tributary of that far from mighty river. It was certainly a water closet but in ecological terms it may have left a little to be desired. Legend had it that an imaginative fifth-former had secreted himself in the first privy inside the door (which was upstream of all the others) and had waited until the rest were occupied before dropping a petrol-soaked rag into the water and following it with a lighted match. The bog may have been a trifle primitive but our gymnasium, a fairly recent and well-found addition to the school, had the latest thing in lavatories — a number of cubicles with the usual offices and a row of those vertical corrugations known as urinals. 'Urinal' is an unattractive word touch of elegance in that each corrugation boasted the manufacturer's logo as an aiming mark. The founder of the firm was either intensely proud of his creation or a master of self-deprecation because his logo was a decorative oval inscribed 'George Jennings — the Closet of the Century'. He would surely have been a worthy business associate of the reputed inventor of the water closet, Mr Thomas Crapper.

Once a year the School O.T.C., the Officer Training Corps, dislocated the Birmingham traffic by marching out to Camp. The Corps paraded in the quadrangle, the mighty oaken gates swung wide and a long column of khaki-clad adolescents headed by the School Band marched out, wheeling left into New Street then right and up Corporation Street to Snow Hill station where we entrained for Tidworth Camp on Salisbury Plain.

The members of the Band were not chosen for musical ability but rather for their size or because of other attributes which rendered them unfit to bear arms. My friend Sidney Lines was over six feet tall and to him was delegated the duty of carrying the Big Drum and wearing the coveted leopard skin. He walloped the drum with enthusiasm whenever he deemed a loud bang to be appropriate. I was rather small and was at first entrusted with a pair of cymbals. Marching with these diabolical contrivances was practically impossible and on one occasion when I inadvertently swung both arms together I was carried forward several feet and impinged on the boy in front. I should probably have carried the damn things chest high, but I didn't know and nobody told me. The Corps was largely trained by Sergeant-Major Moore, one of the gym instructors. Like most warrant officers he was a fine man, adored by the boys and held in some awe because he had a leather-gloved artificial hand — the real one having been shot off in some battle on the western front. I expect he could have advised me about the cymbals but he was more interested in the martial than the musical arts. My hatred for those cymbals knew no bounds and I was secretly relieved when I managed to lose the School an alleged first place in the Band Competition by whanging them together with a frightful clang just after the rest of the Band had completed its programme of so-called music. To my intense joy this little mishap deprived me of the cymbals for good, but as the authorities still thought me an unlikely warrior I was put in charge of a tenor drum. It was about as difficult to march with this thing banging about on my left knee as with the cymbals but my main difficulty remained that I was, and always have been, completely tone deaf. Luckily the noise of a tenor drum is fairly muted, quite unlike the awful clangour of the cymbals, and my untimely thumping passed unnoticed in the general cacophony.

My dispiriting career in the Corps did not deter me from joining the Territorial Army in 1939. Perhaps I was subconsciously inspired by the example of one of our more illustrious Old Boys who ended up as Field-Marshal Lord Slim. Some forty years later our sons were in the same regiment, 22 S.A.S. My Nicolas was a young trooper; Lieutenant-Colonel John Slim, twenty years his senior, was the Commanding Officer.

As far as I can remember my only distinction at school was to win the Reynolds Art Prize by painting a human skull wearing a tasselled First Fifteen Rugby cap, and calling it 'The Old Edwardian'. My Scottish birth ensured that I never understood even the rudiments of cricket, but I enjoyed rugby football and laboriously gained my House Colours and an occasional place in the school second team. I was rather better at Physical Training and my mastery of such mildly acrobatic capers as the back upstart, handspring and flying backlift earned me my School Colours. To my chagrin I could never quite manage the free somersault but my ability to turn a handspring remained with me for many years and even as a consultant surgeon I always ended a dinner dance, whether it was the hospital ball or an evening at the Savoy, by turning a few handsprings and an occasional back upstart on the dance floor. In these days of racial tensions it is worth remembering that every public school used to have one black pupil, always reputed to be the son of a Zulu chief, always called Inky and usually the most popular boy in the school. The Inky of my brothers' day was their great friend and a frequent visitor to our home. I never knew his real name and remember him mainly for his great height, fine looks and the musical timbre of his faultless English. He always won the hundred yards on Sports Day and was noted for the speed with which he could catch cheeky townee urchins and administer summary punishment for shouting 'nigger' at him.

My moderate achievements at school were a source of great disappointment to my father, who had been conditioned to success by the brilliance of my elder brother Athol and the considerable ability of my second brother Leicester, Athol's junior by a couple of years. Athol was captain of rugger, cricket and fives, and effortlessly acquired a long string of scholarships and prizes. My father worshipped him and was heart-broken by the tragedy which ultimately befell him. I was a child when Athol was in his prime and he was a remote figure of whom I was greatly in awe. He set great store by sartorial elegance, never wore what would nowadays be called casual clothes and mostly appeared in perfectly cut formal suits. He wore strange things called spats around his ankles and out of doors he was never without a bowler hat and neatly furled umbrella. Soon after he qualified as a doctor he joined the army. Perhaps the uniform was the attraction. He was posted as a regimental medical officer but his military career was painfully short. A few months after he joined he was discovered to have pulmonary tuberculosis. Tuberculosis, in all its forms, was rife in those days. The layman's name for the pulmonary or lung version was consumption, presumably because it seemed to consume the wasted bodies of the sufferers. It was a terrible disease — another name for it was the white plague — and it carried off a vast number of our young men and women. Always, it seemed, they were the best-looking and the most promising. The infection, by the tubercle

17

bacillus, was spread by droplet infection from the sputum of the sufferers and had the effect of destroying and cavitating the lungs. Doctors made determined, and largely futile, attempts to stem the progress of the disease by collapsing the affected lung, either by crushing the phrenic nerve in the neck to paralyze the diaphragm, injecting air into the chest cavity (artificial pneumothorax) or by the mutilating operation of thoracoplasty. This consisted of removing a number of ribs so that the chest wall fell inwards.

The patients were confined, if possible, in sanatoria – partly for their own good and partly to limit the spread of the disease in the population. The sanatoria were sited at the highest available altitude, where it was thought that the air would be cleaner and healthier. In Switzerland there was actually a 'cure-tax' just for breathing the stuff. There was strict training in 'handkerchief drill' to avoid infecting others, and the patients conformed to a regimen of graduated exercise in the open air. Windows were left open but because direct sunlight was thought to exacerbate the infection they were taught they should see the sun, but the sun should not see them.

All this had little long-term effect on the almost inevitable outcome and they died in their hundreds of thousands. Then, it seemed miraculously, drugs and antibiotics were discovered which actually destroyed the tubercle bacillus and this awful plague was virtually eradicated. It was a great medical triumph, but it was too late for my family and for a great part of whole generations of our young people. Athol told nobody except my parents that he had the disease, and he made no attempt to treat himself. He was invalided out of the army and he borrowed money from my father to buy a general practice. Practices were bought and sold for their goodwill and death vacancies were cheaper than practices whose incumbents were still alive. Athol paid eleven hundred pounds for a death vacancy and, still keeping silent about his disease, worked as a general practitioner until the day he died. He did not encourage visitors and we never saw him, but we were told that he had delivered a baby twenty-four hours before his death. I never really knew him, but I wish I had.

Leicester, in physique and temperament, was quite different from Athol. He was exuberant, a little above average height and immensely powerful, clever, inventive and humorous, a superb artist, a good tennis player and, like Athol, a fine rugger player. He played full back for Birmingham University and his deadly tackles were a sight to behold. He loved general practice and after doing a few locums bought a country practice based on the little village of Turvey in Bedfordshire. He married a lovely and charming girl, Doreen, and we all went to live with him in Turvey. I know now that this was a great mistake. Leicester was my mother's favourite and while my poor father commuted daily from Bedford to his business in Birmingham, my mother lived up to the music-hall parody of a mother-in-law and did little to foster harmony in a household where Doreen should, by rights, have been the mistress.

Domestic discord was soon followed by disaster, for although Leicester was an excellent G.P. and was very popular in the village it became clear in a year or so that he, too, had pulmonary tuberculosis and that his short medical career was over. The practice had to go and it was sold to an old friend, Harold Round. Mother, father and I moved back to Birmingham, while Leicester, Doreen and their daughter Josephine began long years of travail. Warned by Athol's death, Leicester had taken out an insurance policy and had five hundred pounds a year to live on. That was quite a substantial sum in those inflation-free days and although he was treated for a while in Midhurst Sanatorium they spent most of their time in Davos, in Switzerland. Consumptives lived in curious tribal societies united by their common disability and restricted life style, and cocooned from the rest of the world. Leicester and Doreen seemed very happy, always hospitable, always living life to the full and making light of their troubles. One by one their new friends would die off but a few lived on for years. Inexorably, if almost imperceptibly, the progress of these survivors was always downhill.

Away from the sanatoria it was a busy eventful world. I qualified as a doctor in 1935 at the age of twenty-two and started to train as a surgeon, first as a house surgeon at the General Hospital, Birmingham, then as resident surgical officer at the Birmingham Children's Hospital and surgical registrar at the new Queen Elizabeth Hospital. As a student I had watched this magnificent complex being built and had wondered if I would ever be lucky enough to get a job there. In the event I was one of the first batch of residents to be appointed. It was a bit strange; there were no patients and the place was eerily quiet: it didn't even smell like a hospital. The wards and the corridors shone with polish and all the equipment was brand new and unused. The workmen had not quite finished in the residents' quarters but we were glad to see a couple of full-sized snooker tables. That was where I and Alec Innes, the R.S.O., spent our first evening and we polished off a bottle of wine which the Matron had kindly presented to us on arrival. A few weeks later the hospital was officially opened by Queen Elizabeth, now the Queen Mother. We all stood to in our respective wards, the consultants waiting at the door to receive and bow to the Queen and the rest of us, the junior doctors and the nurses, stationed at intervals around the ward. The Prime Minister, Mr Neville Chamberlain, a Birmingham man himself, was part of the Royal retinue and I noticed that he appeared to hang back so that the ripple of applause which greeted the Queen's approach would be followed by a secondary ripple on his own arrival. I was standing in front of a window and when the Queen had dealt with the initial formalities she made a beeline in my direction, her wonderful smile very much in evidence. Still beaming, she came right up to me. I thought it was jolly decent of her to take notice of a junior and I began anxiously to wonder what I should say in reply. She looked out of the window and turned to the Prime Minister. 'Haven't they done well with the gardens?' she said.

When, a couple of years later, Mr Chamberlain declared war on Germany I was an assistant medical officer at the Wellhouse Hospital in Barnet, Herts. In the old days it had been a workhouse and the character of Oliver Twist was said to have been based on one of its inmates. The old workhouse records, great heavy ledgers, were fascinating reading. One of the ledger headings was 'Reason for admission' and a very common entry was the one word 'bastard'. The other entries were equally terse and I remember that one poor chap had earned the comment 'Proved refractory: sent to treadmill'.

In September, 1939, the nation held its breath while Mr Chamberlain made his fateful announcement over the radio. His tone was one of despair but for most of us it was a relief. The waiting and the uncertainty were over: we were at war. The blackout descended and the Territorial Army was embodied. I was posted as regimental medical officer to a Royal Artillery unit in Bristol and my brother, who was in Italy, came home. My departure reduced the surgical staff of the Wellhouse Hospital by one third. The two remaining were Dr H.R. Segar, the Medical Superintendent, and Dr George Brentnall. Dr Segar and his family had a fine house in the hospital grounds. George and I shared a flat with his dog. We were general purpose doctors in those days and the evening before I was called up I removed an appendix, prescribed for a case of lobar pneumonia and delivered a baby. During my six years absence the hospital expanded enormously and when I returned it was a fine 500-bed general hospital. With the advent of the N.H.S. in 1948 its name was changed to Barnet General Hospital and in the fullness of time I was appointed as one of its consultant general surgeons and remained on its staff until I retired in 1973. It was a very happy hospital with a wealth of surgical work and I enjoyed every minute of my time there, profiting greatly from the friendship and example of many skilful and delightful colleagues – both senior and junior, medical, nursing and administrative. Later on I was appointed to the consultant staff of Finchley Memorial Hospital. This was a so-called 'cottage hospital' of a type which, alas, has largely disappeared. We had about sixty beds and quite a large consultant staff, mostly recruited from the London teaching hospitals. We undertook almost every kind of surgery and maintained a twenty-four-hour emergency service with the help of one overworked resident house officer. The local general practitioners, who were of a very high calibre, played a full part in the running of the hospital and, when I first worked there, gave most of the anaesthetics. Later on, as anaesthetic technology became increasingly complex, this work was taken over by the consultant anaesthetists from Barnet General Hospital – where the anaesthetic department, under the leadership of Dr James Rochford, was internationally renowned. The general practitioner who gave my anaesthetics in the early days was Dr Neville Stokoe, whose untimely death a few years later came as a great blow. In life he was quiet, efficient and unassuming, and he maintained those attributes to the very end. He died quietly and unobtrusively in the middle of a rubber of bridge. I remember one of his stories of general practice: he had had as a patient for many years a known hypochondriac who was always complaining of indeterminate symptoms and demanding unnecessary investigations which always failed to show anything seriously amiss. One evening Neville was called out to find the man in bed with vague pains in the chest. Meticulous as always, he examined his patient carefully, found nothing wrong and accepted the offer of a cup of coffee from the patient's wife. 'There's nothing wrong with George, you know,' he said reassuringly. 'Come upstairs and we'll try and talk some sense into him.' They finished their coffee and went up together. George was lying back on his pillow, as dead as a doornail. Neville said that he could think of absolutely nothing to say.

I sympathized with him. I knew the feeling. Early in the war I had, in addition to my main job, the task of looking after the medical needs of a detachment of what was to become the Home Guard. This particular lot was exactly like 'Dad's Army' and one dear old boy came to see me, complaining, like George, of vague pains in his chest. I examined him with the care due to his years, tapped his chest, listened with a stethoscope, felt his pulse and took his blood pressure, and found nothing amiss. While he was dressing I filled in Army Form B.256. Medical officers had to fill in this form every time they saw a patient and it was a curious document which divided patients into three categories described as 'M and D', 'Attend B' and 'Attend C'. I have forgotten the significance of the last two categories but M and D entitled the sufferer to a dose of medicine (M) and a prompt return to duty (D). I regret to say that this was the category in which I placed my old boy. He chattered away about the vegetables in his allotment, buttoned up his battledress blouse, slung his gasmask over his shoulder, set his forage cap at a jaunty angle, gave me a Dad's Army salute ... and dropped dead. My place of work at the time was a Cavalry School and both I and my medical orderly, Corporal Upton, were very much taken aback. We had never had a death on the premises before and were uncertain of the correct procedure. I hastily crossed the M and D off the A.F. B.256 and then we carried the old boy into the kitchen and covered him with a Union Flag. It seemed the decent thing to do. The moral, if any, of these two stories is that a massive heart attack can be preceded by vague pains in the chest, but I hasten to add, for the benefit of any reader who feels a bit of discomfort coming on, that it is a pretty rare event.

However, all this was later on – and down in Bristol in September, 1939, I was unused to military life. I had not been an assiduous Territorial and my only training had been a fortnight's course at the R.A.M.C. Depot in Crookham. Among other useful things I had been taught that by using an instrument called a land auger I could drill down through the ground to the water table, plant a lavatory seat on top of the hole and be the proud owner of a water closet. I never saw this done during the war: we just dug holes of various sizes, but I felt that the idea would have appealed to the chap who built my old school. When I arrived at my unit I was told to inspect the meat in the cookhouse, inspect the latrines and vaccinate the regiment. The meat was half a cow hanging on a hook and it looked all right to me. The so-called latrines were ordinary W.C.s and I pulled a chain or two in a knowing manner: they were all right too. Vaccinating the regiment was something else, and they seemed to want it doing right away. I had never even seen a vaccination nor had I been vaccinated myself. I had no books and there was no real doctor around to ask. However, I knew the principles of the thing: I knew that you had to scarify an area of skin and apply the lymph to the scarified area. Casting my mind back to football changing rooms I remembered that some of my friends had a pattern of four scars each about the size of a sixpence on their upper arms. O.K., I thought, I'll get to work. I laboriously scarified the four circles on each man's arm and rubbed the lymph well in. It took ages and we had to send for some more lymph but I got it done in the end. There was a seven-day calm before the storm; then all hell broke loose. The regiment went down as if it had been pole-axed. The poor boys had temperatures of 103°F. or more and black gangrenous holes appeared in some of my 'sixpences'. We were a Territorial regiment and a lot of the chaps lived at home. Anxious mothers telephoned to say that 'Johnny wasn't very well and wouldn't be coming in today'. I travelled all over Bristol seeing my victims and luckily nobody died. It was weeks before the regiment could muster at full strength, but this truly appalling mistake did my reputation a lot of good. It was felt that the regiment had a real doctor — a chap who didn't do things by halves. Months later the official instructions for vaccination arrived: I should have made a linear scratch a quarter of an inch long instead of those awful sixpences. I tore the instruction up.

I was so upset by all this that I asked my C.O., Lieutenant-Colonel Reginald Carey Ames, for forty-eight hours leave. He seemed to want a reason so I said, 'To get married,' feeling that it was none of his business. To my astonishment he explained that in the army one does not marry without the Commanding Officer's permission and that it was considered desirable for him to vet one's fiancée. Thea was a very high-spirited girl and I didn't think this was a frightfully good idea — but she did. The Mess Secretary laid on a party in the large house we occupied in Bristol. Thea looked absolutely splendid and was an immediate hit; the waiters, who didn't know her as well as I did, saw that her glass was replenished at regular intervals and later on in the evening she disappeared. I was chatting uneasily with the Colonel and getting rather worried when she materialized on the balcony, a sort of minstrel's gallery, above our heads. Nothing wrong with that, but she was wearing the Colonel's pyjamas and clutching his framed King's Commission which, oddly enough, he kept hanging on a wall of the room which he used as part office, part bedroom. I was pretty used to Thea's outrageous ways but this seemed to be carrying things a great deal too far. Worse was to come. She began, in a loud clear voice, to read out his Commission to the startled gathering below. She had got as far as 'To Our Trusty and Well Beloved Reginald Carey Ames, Greetings!' when I reached her.

I wasn't exactly sober myself and nor was the Colonel, but I have never quite understood the details of that evening's entertainment. However, the upshot of it all was that we were married in a Bristol Registry Office which was still permeated by the heady perfume of an actress whose nuptials had preceded ours. My best man was our great friend Captain John Bishop who was stationed not far away as M.O. to the 50th Royal Tank Regiment. We had qualified together and were both training as surgeons when the war began, but he had the misfortune to lose his left arm in the battle of El Alamein, and when the war was over had to choose between becoming a psychiatrist or a radiologist. To my intense relief he chose the latter. We gave a reception of sorts at the Grand Hotel and the Regiment presented us with a silver salver engraved with the signatures of all the officers. It remains one of our treasured possessions, and the final tribute to Thea's balcony scene was the Colonel's award of seven days leave instead of the customary forty-eight hours. Quite a girl, my wife.

Before the regiment went abroad I was posted to the Equitation School at Weedon, then to 152 Field Ambulance, then briefly to an Airborne Field Ambulance, then promoted to major and posted as a company commander to 185 Field Ambulance attached to 128 Infantry Brigade (The Hampshire Brigade). With them I landed in North Africa and, later, on the beaches at Salerno. After the terrible crossing of the River Rapido at Cassino I was promoted again to lieutenant-colonel as officer commanding No 1 Field Ambulance attached to the 1st Guards Brigade. I was still with them in January, 1945, when my dear wife took a hand in my affairs.

The big battles in Italy were over, the Guards were holding their section of the line in the north of Italy, and I was doing nothing in particular. At home all was far from well with my family. Father had died, Thea had had a major abdominal operation but had taken my mother, now slightly dotty, into our London flat in Dolphin Square – and my brother was dying in Birmingham. Thea felt that matters had come to a pretty pass and that something must be done about it. Being Thea she felt that the right thing to do would be to write to Winston Churchill. After all, she reasoned, he was the chap in charge and would surely know what to do. She told him that I would be much more use at home than messing about in Italy and that I ought to see my brother before he died. Mr Churchill had a few pressing matters on his mind at that particular time, but, incredibly, he took note of Thea's problems and replied by return of post. He told her to take his letter to General Hood, the Director-General of Medical Services, and she did. She has always regretted that in the stress of the moment she forgot to ask for her letter back. It would have been a wonderful memento of a great man's consideration and kindness.

I knew nothing about all this and was astonished to receive a signal posting me home. The date was 25 January, 1945, and I had only a few days to hand over to my second-in-command and to make my goodbyes. My last call was on Lieutenant-Colonel John Nelson, O.C. 3rd Bn, the Grenadier Guards. His battalion headquarters was in some sort of farmhouse and he was taking his ease in a stable, half-sitting, half-lying in a manger filled with straw.

'I'm going home,' I said.

'Why?'

'Compassionate posting.'

'You bloody shit,' he said amiably.

On the way back to my own H.Q. we had to pass a point which was regularly shelled with Teutonic precision. It was no great problem: one simply stopped one's jeep a hundred yards or so short of the target area, waited for a shell to come in and then drove on. Krauts were creatures of habit and there was no chance of them sending in another shell before the appointed time. Nevertheless, as my driver slowed to a halt and we watched a burning hut which had been set alight by a previous salvo I felt a little nervous. Just suppose that for once, when I was going home, the silly nits varied their routine. They didn't, the expected shell arrived and we drove on. That was the last loud bang I heard in the Second World War.

I embarked at Naples on 28 January and we had a wonderful trip home. We were a very mixed bunch, all in the best of spirits. The actress Pauline Jameson was one of the passengers and was the cynosure of many woman-starved eyes. I shared a cabin with an army surgeon and a bottle of whisky. The bottle was his but he was a very pleasant and hospitable man. There was a concert every night with some star performances from the passengers, and when we disembarked on 22 February I felt that we had had a splendid pleasure cruise. I caught a train to London, made my way to Dolphin Square and rang the bell of our flat. Thea opened the door and we fell into each other's arms. It was a little time before she told me that Leicester had been buried the day before.

An Oddity of Patients

Naughty, some of them, but nice

The waiting room was large, and it was full. The patients sat in rows, and if they talked at all it was in hushed whispers to their neighbours. The receptionist was a kindly, bustling, authoritarian and rather stout woman who issued stentorian orders from time to time. An elderly couple was sitting at the end of the second row, and when it came to the old gentleman's turn to be examined she called his name loudly and told him to go into a cubicle and get undressed.

'Go and help him,' she added to the old lady and the pair tottered into the cubicle together. When the consultant went in, the old boy was lying stark naked on the couch, his clothes were piled neatly on one of the two chairs in the cubicle, and the old lady was sitting on the other with her hands primly folded in her lap. The examination was not very productive, for the old gentleman was a poor witness and deaf into the bargain. The slightly exasperated surgeon turned to the old lady for help.

'How long has your husband had this pain in his hip?'

'Husband!' she said, 'I've never seen him before in me life.'

If anyone should think that this old bird, whom I came to know quite well, was a bit silly or even a little forward in her docile application to the task of undressing a total stranger, let them ponder their own sheeplike behaviour in, say, an airport. In unfamiliar surroundings the vast majority of us do as we are told without question, and in our ordered society we are being told to do something, or not to do something, most of the time. It is surprising how many parts we play in the course of a day, and how many appellations we attract. In a very few hours one and the same

27

person can be a motorist, pedestrian, passenger, client, customer and, if unlucky, patient. Some doctors seem temporarily to forget that patients are people, and give them yet another name: 'cases'. Sometimes they are promoted to be 'interesting cases'. How can persons be, in this sense, cases? They are individuals and the very least they deserve is to be described as such. In my letters to other doctors I often referred to my patients as old ruins, little poppets, little horrors, miserable old sods and charming old birds ... but as 'cases', never. Even famous doctors can slip into this medical vernacular. Sir Arthur Conan Doyle was a doctor before he was an author and it is not altogether surprising that Sherlock Holmes was always banging on about his 'interesting cases'. It is fitting that the character of this most famous fictional sleuth was conceived in the wards of the Edinburgh Royal Infirmary. It was here that medical students, including the young Conan Doyle, were fascinated by the deductive methods of Joseph Bell, one of the hospital surgeons. These methods became those of Sherlock Holmes, and indeed they were once quite common among doctors, though they have now given place to strings of scientific investigations which are more accurate but far less entertaining.

Even now it is sometimes possible to baffle a patient and perhaps raise his or her opinion of one's clinical acumen by a very simple observation. I was examining a woman's abdomen one day and remarked without preamble, 'I see that you are very fond of jugged hare.' She agreed that she was, and seemed duly puzzled and impressed. I am afraid this was no stroke of deductive genius on my part: it was 'elementary'. The clue, which the patient knew nothing about, was in the X-ray. This showed a small collection of lead shot in a position which made it almost certain that they were in the appendix. This is quite common and nearly always leads to trouble in the end. A friend of mine had to operate, in peacetime, on a major-general whose appendix was packed solid with lead. The gallant officer owned a large estate, was a keen shot and very addicted to pheasant. My patient obviously liked game and might have been an inveterate pheasant-eater, but I guessed at jugged hare and happened to be right. Another time I managed to gain the confidence of a very large lady by asking after her budgerigar.

'He's fine,' she said, 'but how on earth did you know I'd got a budgerigar?'

I didn't like to tell her, but again it was a very simple explanation. Her navel was full of bird seed. I suppose that when she reached up to replenish the little chap's feeding bowl some of the bird seed slipped out of her fingers and down the front of her dress, which would have been held forward in a receptive and supplicant attitude by her ample bosom, with its central channel leading directly to her navel.

When I was a medical student I had the privilege of working for a distinguished Midland surgeon. At the time I thought him a pompous old fellow, but as the years went by I realized that he was a man of infinite wisdom. One of his dicta was that if you perform any operation however simple a thousand times, something will go wrong at least once: not necessarily anything seriously wrong, but something. The lesson he was trying to teach is that one must be eternally vigilant, however trivial the procedure appears to be. How right he was. One cannot imagine any procedure less alarming than taking the body temperature with a clinical thermometer, but twice I have had to perform an abdominal operation as a direct result of this commonplace investigation. The first arose from a fairly common error: a child's temperature was taken with the thermometer in his mouth instead of in his armpit. The child bit the end off the thermometer and swallowed the bulb, the piece containing the mercury. Children often swallow stray objects, and nine times out of ten the article completes its long and tortuous journey through the intestinal tract and ends up in the lavatory pan ... but we had to operate on my little chap because the fragment lodged in his appendix and gave him acute appendicitis. The same problem, really, as the major-general and his pheasants.

Like all surgeons, I have operated many times for the removal of swallowed foreign bodies, sometimes because they stayed put in the stomach for many days, and sometimes because a sharp object perforated the gut, though alarming items like needles and open safety pins can, on occasion, complete the whole journey safely. Now and again great lumps of bolted food may cause a complete obstruction of the bowel. I have removed a whole peeled orange for this reason, and another time a gooey mass containing nine date stones and a silver sixpence. One of my colleagues boasts that he is the only surgeon to have removed a London bus from a child's stomach. Toys like that and most other items are swallowed accidentally, but some pretty strange things are swallowed on purpose. I recall one attractive young woman whose persistent vomiting was thought at first to be the result of a dietary indiscretion. She had eaten oysters and taken a good deal of whisky the night before, but later it appeared that there was something more seriously amiss – and at operation we found the bowel stopped up by an accumulated mass of string. The next day she readily admitted that she had been in the habit of eating string since childhood, and had not thought the fact worth mentioning. Lunatic asylums sometimes present the surgeon with a similar problem in the shape of a 'rubbish eater'. These people will eat anything and it is a rather dangerous aberration. I have a photograph showing 110 objects found at autopsy in the intestine of a rubbish eater. They included lengths of chain, coins, corset stiffeners, pipe cleaners and pieces of wood and wire. It was one of the latter which had pierced the bowel and caused the patient's death. One of our regular customers was a likeable young man whose speciality was swallowing triangular pieces of tin which he had shaped to his liking with a pair of shears. On one of his many admissions he was found also to be suffering from a large boil on his bottom. The solicitous ward sister applied a soothing kaolin poultice, and he ate that too.

My second 'disappearing thermometer' incident was more bizarre than the first, and caused a great deal of embarrassment to the charming girl involved. She was married, but for some reason was unable to become pregnant. Under these circumstances my gynaecologist colleagues would sometimes arrange for the patient to keep a chart of her vaginal temperature to determine the time of ovulation. This chart was the cause of the trouble. It was Sunday morning and my patient-to-be and her husband were lying late abed. For obvious reasons there was no patter of tiny feet to disturb their well-earned rest. Dimly she remembered her duty to keep this curious temperature chart and drowsily she stretched out a hand to find the thermometer and pop it into place. She turned over and drifted back to sleep: her bladder was a bit full but it could wait. An hour or so later she reluctantly decided that it could not wait any longer and she threw back the bedclothes. Panic! The thermometer? Where was it? One thing for sure, it wasn't where it should have been. She awakened her husband: they searched the bed and under the bed but there was no thermometer: it had vanished, and in due course she arrived at the hospital. Blushing furiously and very engagingly she recounted the details of the mystery, and the solution was not hard to find. The thermometer was not exactly lost: an X-ray showed it in her bladder. She had popped it into the wrong hole, a mistake anyone could make under the circumstances. We have an instrument, a kind of telescope, for inspecting the interior of the bladder and, sure enough, there was the thermometer. I could even read the temperature on the scale but whenever I tried to grasp the end of the elusive little glass tube with my remote control forceps it slipped away, and I was afraid of breaking it. So for the second time I had to carry out an abdominal operation to retrieve a missing thermometer. She was out of hospital in a week, chastened, still charming and determined to be more careful in the future. Talking of wrong holes it is surprising how many young ladies are not fully conversant with the details of their downstairs anatomy. One of our gynaecologists at the hospital, who was responsible for the training of student midwives, used to ask them to draw on paper a worm's eye view of what they imagined their own arrangements to be. Occasionally she let me see the results and I can tell you some of the drawings were worthy of Picasso at his most obscure.

The replies of patients to apparently innocuous questions can be disconcerting and may leave one at a loss for an adequate response. I knew a lot of my customers by their first names, and Ada was a fat jolly woman with a very loud voice. I had removed her breast for a growth and when I went into the ward the next day she was in a bed on the right hand side. I always started my round on the left hand side, but I was fond of Ada and I called across to her, 'You all right, Ada?'

Her reply was a stentorian bellow which could hardly be regarded as a morale-booster for the rest of my patients.

'Christ!' she yelled, 'You 'aven't arf buggered me up.'

Another woman whom I saw in the out-patient clinic was a lugubrious soul at the best of times.

'How are you getting on?' I asked.

'It's me back: it's bad again.'

I nodded sympathetically. She fixed me with an accusing eye.

'And me brother was murdered this morning!'

What on earth can one say to a conversation-stopper like that? 'What rotten luck'? or 'Just fancy'? Her priorities were a bit odd too.

In my first resident post as a newly qualified doctor I was called to the Casualty Department to see a hen-pecked little man who had difficulty in passing his water. He sat despondently on a chair and his huge domineering wife did all the talking. She jerked a thumb in his direction.

''E's got a stoppage in 'is pipe.'

'And how,' I asked, 'do you know that?'

She looked at me contemptuously: 'Because this afternoon another lady and me blowed up it, o' course.'

I have often wondered who 'the other lady' was, and how she was persuaded to undertake such a fearsome investigation.

Not long after this, it was in 1935, a prisoner was brought to see me. He came from Winson Green prison and was accompanied by two warders. He had a large boil on his bottom, and as was the custom in those days I froze the boil with ethyl chloride spray and lanced it. While the nurse applied a dressing I turned to one of the warders and asked quietly, 'What is he in for?'

'Murder,' said the warder stolidly. 'He's being hanged tomorrow.'

Children are the most delightful of patients. They reply simply and truthfully to questions and the maladies which afflict them are seldom, at any rate from the viewpoint of the general surgeon, very serious. The death of a child would be a terrible tragedy, but fortunately the operations which we are required to perform on them are nearly always straightforward and successful. A children's ward is a noisy, bustling and happy place. I used to do a lot of circumcisions because, unlike some of my contemporaries, I believed it to be a good idea. I remember a fair-haired little boy who had just come round from the anaesthetic. He put one hand confidingly in mine, pointed with the other to his dressing and asked, 'How did it happen?'

This is no place to debate the merits and demerits of circumcision, but it is an historical fact that the operation was brought into disrepute in this country by a learned article in a 1949 issue of the *British Medical Journal*. One of the points made by its author, a distinguished paediatrician, was that all the benefits of circumcision could be conferred by simple cleanliness. In the same year an editorial in one of our national daily papers bemoaned the fact that thirty per cent of the population of Greater London had no bathroom and sixteen per cent had to share a kitchen sink. I suppose things may be a bit better now, but at the time it seemed to me that my paediatrician colleague had taken too rosy a view of the state of the nation's hygiene. A middle-class foreskin could doubtless be cleansed with both assiduity and decorum, but it would require a considerable degree of agility and sangfroid to maintain a similar standard of cleanliness in someone else's kitchen sink.

Mention of circumcision turns my thoughts to urine specimens, and to a patient of mine who had no reason to be grateful for my services. I wanted him to provide a full day's output of urine for examination in the laboratory, but I forgot to give him the sterilised container into which he should have passed his offerings on the following day. However, he was a conscientious man: he had been told to bring us all the urine he passed in the next twenty-four hours, and he did. He returned clutching a decorative chamber pot, nearly full to the brim.

'Good Lord!' I said. 'Did you walk through the streets with that?'

'I did,' he said resentfully. 'They wouldn't let me on the bus.'

Still on the subject of urine specimens: Eric, a splendid chap who used to be one of my house surgeons and is now a consultant pathologist, spent a short time in his younger days as a ship's doctor on a passenger liner. He was the junior doctor and his boss, a Scotsman, was an old hand with much experience of shipboard medicine. On Eric's first working day aboard a large middle-aged American lady called on him in the sick bay.

'I wanna urinalysis,' she demanded.

'Why?'

'I just wanna urinalysis, okay?'

'All right,' said Eric, 'if you insist.'

He made the necessary arrangements to collect the specimen and took it to his Scottish boss.

'Some old American bird wants her wee examined.'

'Did ye get the two guineas?'

'No.'

'Well, go and get it.'

Very reluctantly Eric sought out his patient, collected the fee and returned to his superior.

'I've got the two guineas. What do I do with the specimen?'

'Throw it in the sink.'

Readers who set some store by the conventions of polite discourse may have noticed that the general tone of this narrative has gone from bad to worse. I have reluctantly to report that it is going to get even more dispiriting. It is a sad fact, and not at all my fault, that many of the more intriguing and anecdotal facets of medicine are concerned with what my ten-year-old grandson calls his personal parts. The general public can have no idea of the insults to which personal parts can be subjected, and as a young medical student nor had I, at least not until I fell in with the late Mr X. I call him Mr X because I can't remember his name or even his general appearance. He was certainly the cynosure of all eyes, but they were riveted on a part of his anatomy which is not generally on public view. It was, however, intimately concerned with Mr X's life, and death. He worked in a local factory and his troubles stemmed from a bad habit of pressing very unwelcome attentions on his female colleagues. They banded together and determined to teach him a sharp lesson. The factory was part of a light engineering concern which manufactured, among other items, large steel washers, and while some of the irate ladies overpowered our patient-to-be and held him down, the others threaded a dozen or so washers over the offending member of his personal parts. By the time he reached hospital the tissues had swollen, and the washers could not be pulled off. The startled surgeon was faced with what amounted to a steel tube some five inches long with walls about half an inch thick. The problem was beyond his capacity to resolve, and the hospital engineer was called in consultation. The engineer was even more taken aback than the surgeon: he was not accustomed to dealing with flesh and blood, and he retired to his workshop in an effort to concentrate his mind. After a due interval he emerged, looking none too optimistic, with a selection of hacksaws and power-driven grinding wheels. The washers were eventually removed but the damage was appalling and the poor man died of a spreading infection. This was in the days before antibiotics, and if they had been available I dare say he would have survived.

I have seen other sad little experiments with this part of the anatomy which have also led to a fatal outcome; but most situations in this area, however bizarre or unusual, can be retrieved without physical injury and with only temporary embarrassment to the patient's *amour propre*. The conjunction of an enquiring mind and a fertile imagination can result in some memorable eccentricities. One young man who came briefly under my care had whiled away an idle afternoon in a manner which must surely be unique. First he borrowed his mother's forcing bag from the kitchen. A forcing bag is normally used when icing cakes and is a large conical bag made out of strong cotton cloth with a metal or plastic nozzle fitted into the apex of the cone. Pastry cooks fill the bag with sugar icing and force or squirt the contents in decorative fashion over the surface of the cake. That is what pastry cooks do, but our hero had other ideas. He put the pilfered forcing bag in a safe place and repaired to a chemist's where be bought an ample supply of plaster of Paris. He mixed the plaster with water according to the instructions in the packet, filled Mum's bag with the mixture, and squirted the whole lot into his back passage. By the time he arrived, rather crestfallen, at the hospital the plaster of Paris had set into a solid block about six inches long and four inches in diameter. Its removal was clearly going to be a rather malodorous enterprise, and I delegated it to a heavily masked subordinate while giving encouragement from a safe distance in the theatre doorway.

Another young man with time on his hands spent three months sewing his wife's hair, one hair at a time, through the dependent element of his personal parts with a darning needle. I never asked these adventurous spirits why they indulged in such extraordinary activities. I doubt if I would have got a very coherent answer, and surely each quaint little gambit must have seemed the right thing to do at the time.

I looked into the operating theatre one day and was surprised to see a colleague sitting on a stool and gazing at an anaesthetized patient from whose behind protruded the handle of what appeared to be an iron poker.

'What on earth have you put that in for?' I enquired.

'I haven't,' he said indignantly 'I'm trying to get it out'

He waggled it to show me. 'It seems to be stuck.'

Just then the senior surgeon arrived, and the three of us remained lost in thought for a few minutes. We had long ceased to wonder why people do these strange things to their own persons, but we were baffled as to why the poker would not emerge the way it had gone in. The senior surgeon drew on his vast experience of human anatomy and eccentricity, and suddenly inspiration came to him.

'I've got it!'

His explanation was little short of genius. The human rectum is not, as one might suppose, a simple tube. It is designed, for reasons we need not go into, like a spiral staircase – and the poker was one of those old-fashioned devices with an end shaped like a giant corkscrew. The patient had literally screwed the poker into his behind.

'Turn it to the right,' said the senior surgeon.

The poker went further in.

'Now turn it to the left.'

Success! Out it came.

Not all unseemly situations are the result of misplaced human endeavour. Some befall the patient very much against his will. There is a very distressing phenomenon known as persistent priapism, in which the victim is suddenly seized with a massive erection of his personal parts. Instead of subsiding after a due and decent interval the erection persists, sometimes for many days, to the great confusion and embarrassment of the sufferer. The cause of this affliction is usually obscure and in my experience time is the only healer. However, all sorts of expedients from spinal anaesthesia to hypnosis have been tried in efforts to achieve a speedier relief of the patient's distress. I remember a soldier being brought into a military hospital with this affliction, and the ribald comments of his fellow squaddies did very little for his peace of mind. All treatment was to no avail and in desperation a message was sent to another hospital where a member of the psychiatric staff was said to be experienced in hypnosis. The psychiatrist arrived, and to everyone's consternation turned out to be a woman. Worse than that, she was extraordinarily pretty and when she sat down on the bed and turned her lovely eyes on the scarlet-faced sufferer with his enormous phallus swaying gently from side to side like a metronome, I felt sure that the patient was far more likely to hypnotise the psychiatrist than the other way round.

My experience as a medical student convinced me that I had no future as an obstetrician, and I saw very little of pregnant ladies from then on. However, pregnancy sometimes obtrudes by chance into the orbit of the general surgeon. It is an astounding fact that women can on rare occasions go to full term and into labour without realizing that they are pregnant. It is difficult to believe this until one has seen it happen, and when it does the lady is apt to present herself at a hospital casualty department complaining merely of abdominal colic. I recall one such occasion vividly. The young lady with the pain, who had seen no reason to involve herself in the formalities of marriage, was accompanied by her mother, a large and solicitous soul who was invited to make herself comfortable in the waiting room while her daughter was examined. The result of this examination galvanized the staff into feverish activity. The girl was well advanced in labour and a blessed event was imminent. The house surgeon and the casualty nurse hastily promoted themselves to obstetrician and midwife respectively, and they did a very good job, shepherding a healthy male infant into a rather unprepared world in double quick time. The child was wrapped up and put in an improvised crib by the side of the couch, the examination cubicle was tidied up and a junior nurse despatched to tell the patient's mother, now elevated to the rank of grandmother, that she could go in and see her daughter. The daughter was sitting bolt upright on the couch. Her eyes were bright, but not with mother love, and she pointed a quivering finger at the crib.

''Ave yer seen it, then?'

The newly created grandmother peered into the crib.

'What's that?' she said.

'It's mine!'

The grandmother swooned, and in falling was unlucky enough

to strike her head on an oxygen cylinder. She sustained mild concussion, and we admitted the whole trio – twittering mother, drowsy infant and unconscious grandmama.

Another event, far from blessed, brought me in the end to the Law Courts as a witness against a man accused of causing grievous bodily harm. A little girl was brought to the hospital in a pitiable state; she had been severely battered about the head and there was a livid mark encircling her neck where her assailant had tried to strangle her with one of her own stockings. She was six months pregnant and it transpired that the man who had made these vicious attacks upon her was also the father of the child. The patient, in fact, was little more than a child herself; she was just twelve years old. It so happened that, on the day the girl was brought in, a newly qualified and rather dour young Scotsman was staying with us. Before dinner I recounted the details of this horrifying crime. He listened impassively and sipped his drink while I described the girl's dreadful injuries, but when I said that she was pregnant his Calvinistic Scottish soul had finally had enough. He put down his drink and with a face like thunder he spoke for the first time: 'D'ye mean he'd tampered wi' her?'

I assured him with equal solemnity that it was as bad a case of tampering as I'd ever seen.

Consultant physicians frequently visit patients in their homes to reinforce or elaborate on the general practitioner's diagnosis and to advise on treatment. These domiciliary visits are not so applicable to surgical practice, and I finally abandoned them after a humiliating scene in a semi-detached and rather undesirable residence in North London. I had been called in to examine a very elderly gentleman with suspected disease of the prostate gland. This condition necessitates examination of the patient's back passage with a gloved finger and after the usual courtesies had been observed the old boy was arranged on the bed, lying on his side with his naked behind presented for my edification and attention. The bed was very low and sagged deeply in the middle so that he appeared to be lying in a sort of trench. Two long lengths of electric flex trailed from a socket on the opposite wall to his bedside lamp and to a small radio. A large and vociferous, if rather incoherent, parrot was shifting about uneasily on a perch just behind and to my right. I drew on my rubber glove and advanced purposefully toward my patient. The electric wires were looped untidily on the beside rug. I tripped over them and hurtled through the air to land heavily on top of the unfortunate and entirely unsuspecting old man, and the parrot, complete with the perch which had got entangled in the wire, landed on top of me. I have never since that awful day done another domiciliary visit.

A hospital is a busy community of souls, and many of the daily events have nothing to do with sickness. The Secretary of one of the hospitals where I worked was a delightful man. Nothing was too much trouble and when it was brought to his notice that a patient, a frail old chap, had inadvertently flushed his false teeth down the lavatory he arranged for the main drain to be opened and personally supervised the salvage of the missing dentures. They were soon discovered up against the grid which had been installed to catch stray objects. Oddly enough there was also another set of teeth, dirty and blackened, which looked as though it had been there undetected for years. Both sets were retrieved, the dirty old blackened set consigned to the incinerator and the others washed, wrapped in tissue paper, and returned to the old gentleman. His fumbling fingers slowly undid the wrappings while the smiling Hospital Secretary waited by the bedside to be commended.

'No, mate,' said the old chap at last. 'This lot ain't my teef. Mine was a dirty old black set.'

Au Secours!

Hints on First Aid

On our way to Alsace we stopped for the night in Compiègne. On holiday Thea likes to choose an hotel from the *Guide Michelin* as we drive along, and she had settled on a small place with a 'three knives and forks' rating for good food. We went in together and I opened negotiations with the receptionist in my halting French.

'*Est-ce-que vous avez une chambre à deux lits?*'

We always ask for twin beds because I am rather a restless sleeper, but I have never seen any reason to advertise this marital frailty. However, on this occasion Thea, whose French is only marginally better than mine, saw fit to explain our preference in specific detail.

'*Mon mari,*' she said, '*est très actif dans la nuit.*'

The receptionist, a dark-haired bespectacled spinsterish-looking woman of indeterminate age, had been looking down at her bookings, but now her head jerked up and she fixed me with a steely gaze which raked me from head to foot. She evidently hadn't bargained on providing accommodation for a middle-aged sex maniac. What she saw must have reassured her because her expression slowly relaxed. It was clear that she didn't see me in the role of a rapist. I felt slightly diminished by her almost contemptuous assessment of my potential but we were pleased enough to get the room.

The hotel had been justly commended for its food but the general decor was poor: it owed little to art and a good deal to the tortured imagination of the local handyman. I looked round at the other guests in the dining-room, partly out of interest and partly to get my eyes off the wallpaper. At the next table a heavily built German was drinking soup through a huge drooping moustache. It was not a pleasant sight and even his frau, an ample grey-haired woman, averted her gaze. While we waited for our next course Thea asked me to go up to our room for a packet of cigarettes and on my way back I stopped, aghast, at the top of the last flight of stairs. The German was no longer in the dining-room: he was flat on his back in the foyer, with his wife and a couple of waiters bending over his prostrate form. I knew what had happened: he'd had a heart attack, and I ought to dash down the stairs and try to revive him. This would include mouth-to-mouth resuscitation and I thought of the soup and that awful moustache. I hovered uncertainly on the landing but I didn't know that Thea had come to the same diagnosis and had reassured the assembled company that her husband was a doctor and would undoubtedly put everything to rights as soon as he got back. She has a bad habit of recommending my services to all and sundry. One of the waiters looked up and saw me.

'*M'sieu!*' he shouted, '*Au secours! Vite!*'

There was no escape, and I joined the little tableau in the foyer. The dreadful moustache was still liberally anointed with potage and I eyed it apprehensively while I felt the German's pulse. To my infinite relief the beat was still present, and most important of all it was slow. The worthy Herr was suffering not from a heart attack but from a simple faint — what we in the trade call a vaso-vagal attack. In a real heart attack the pulse, if present at all, would have been feeble and rapid.

Whatever poets may say to the contrary the heart is not the fount of love, nor the spleen the seat of anger. The heart is just a simple four-chambered pump put in to shift ten pints of blood round and round the body. Like some other mechanical pumps it has an accelerator and a brake, and its brake is part of the vagus nerve. The word 'vagus' means 'wandering', and this interesting and important nerve starts off in the brain and meanders down through the neck and chest, where it sends connections to the heart, and on into the abdomen where it sends other connections to the stomach. The functions of the brain, the heart and the stomach are therefore closely linked and simple fainting attacks are often due to some affront to the mind or the stomach. Winning the pools or the

41

thought of having an injection would come into the first category, and drinking ice cold fluid on an empty stomach or diving into a swimming pool after a heavy meal would come into the second. Any such affront can over-stimulate the vagus nerve and as a result the heart slows right down, the blood pressure falls, the supply of blood to the brain is reduced and the sufferer falls unconscious to the ground. In the case of our German friend I strongly suspected an overdose of hot soup on an empty stomach, and after a few minutes he scrambled to his feet and went up to his bedroom. His wife could not have noticed my hesitation on the landing and she must have commended my concern, for when they returned to the dining room he presented me with an enormous cigar. However, the memory of that soup-encrusted moustache lingers on and I now keep in my car a device which would allow me to carry out artificial respiration without any mouth-to-mouth contact.

Before we leave the vagus nerve to its wanderings, I would like to recount the minor role it played at a dinner served in far more elegant surroundings than those of the affair in Compiègne. I had operated on Freddy, a Cambridge don, and he very kindly invited me to dine with him in Jesus College, where he was very famous and much loved. The dinner was excellent and the wines out of this world, but I didn't really fit into the pattern of academic life. A well known historian joined us in Freddy's rooms before we all assembled in the anteroom, and he told me in rather a conspiratorial way that the quality of dinner guests had fallen off very badly in recent years. I murmured sympathetically. He was carrying a copy of the guest list and he pointed to a name.

'Who on earth,' he said, 'is this chap?'

'That's me,' I said, and he did have the grace to look a bit embarrassed, but it was a bad start. After a glass of champagne in the anteroom we went into Hall and were ensconced at the high table. I was struck not only by the beauty of the surroundings but also by the perishing cold. Freddy had omitted to warn me about this but he now confided that he was wearing long woollen drawers, two vests, two pairs of socks and, to my astonishment, Wellington boots under his evening dress. I sat on Freddy's left, and on his right there was a very elderly gentleman, an ex-Provost of Eton, who soon began to feel the whistling draughts so badly that the waiters surrounded him with screens – and that was the last we saw or heard of him. On my left was a distinguished physician, Lord Cohen of Birkenhead. I tried to engage him in conversation, but contrary to popular opinion we doctors never talk shop at dinner, and anyway his shop was different from mine. We fell to discussing our leisure pursuits and he told me that his hobby was collecting jade. He asked what I did with my spare time and I said that I raced motorcars. We struggled for a moment or two to find some link, however tenuous, between the price of jade and the merits of a high-lift camshaft but there was none, and the conversation languished. A pity, because he had a great reputation as an after dinner speaker.

I had now established myself pretty firmly as an academic nonentity with nothing worthwhile to say, but dear old Freddy chattered on amiably and hospitably. The other dons seemed to be a touch parochial and I'm sure that if someone had mentioned Mao Tse Tung they would have said, 'Can't place him. What year was he up?'

At the end of the meal a large silver salver containing a little iced water was passed round, and each diner dipped a finger in the water and wetted the skin behind his ear.

'Why are you doing that?' I asked the don opposite me.

'Because we've always done it.'

I got the feeling that if something had always been done at Jesus, that was justification and explanation enough for anyone, but I battled on. I might not be an academic, but at least I knew the origins of this time-honoured rite and I was prepared to share the knowledge with those around me. A tiny connection of the vagus nerve, I told them, supplies the skin behind the ear, and stimulation of that area, as by a little ice or iced water, can jerk the whole vagus nerve into action – and those fibres which supply the stomach will cause it to contract and expel its contents. In other words, the chap whose ear is being tickled will vomit. This odd discovery was made accidentally many years ago by a greedy old man at a mayoral banquet and the little nerve behind the ear came to be known as 'the alderman's nerve'. The theoretical object of the exercise was to eat a large meal, then nip out to the privy, tickle the back of the ear, throw up and come back for more. However, I don't think that the trick really works unless the stomach is already full to overflowing, and although the silver salver had completed its journey round the table there was no sign of my fellow diners either leaving abruptly or throwing up on the spot. My explanation had done nothing for the appreciation of a superb meal or for the elegance of an old tradition, and it might have been more seemly if I had allowed its origins to remain decently shrouded in the mists of time. On the other hand, perhaps I achieved a kind of immortality: in later years dons may have said to each other at the end of dinner, 'Do you remember that awful chap ...?'

One never knows when one is going to be confronted by a total stranger in the throes of a heart attack, and I always offer up a silent prayer that it will turn out to be a self-curing affront to the vagus nerve rather than the real thing ... or worst of all, a cardiac arrest. In the old days when a patient had a cardiac arrest we were expected to carry out open heart massage after making an incision into either the chest or the abdomen. This rather messy procedure has been superseded for a good many years by external heart massage. The old method required the services of a trained surgeon and was very bad for the nerves of any untrained spectators. The new idea is much simpler and can be carried out by almost anyone who has taken the trouble to swot up the technique in a manual of first aid. To be effective the so-called massage must be performed with the patient lying on a firm surface, which in practice usually means the floor. The front of the chest is then pressed sharply and rhythmically downwards and this procedure is alternated with little bouts of mouth-to-mouth ventilation of the patient's lungs. There's a bit more to it, but that is the essence of the thing.

Even this simple procedure can have totally unexpected and embarrassing consequences. On a cold winter's night some years ago, one of our resident anaesthetists had been dining out with friends, but he was a conscientious chap and when he got back to the hospital he thought he would check up on his patients for the next morning's operating session. He strolled into the relevant female ward and was chatting up the night nurse when one of the patients gave a little cry and collapsed. The nurse helped him to lift the woman on to the floor and then sprinted back to the ward office to press the button for the emergency resuscitation team.

While she was away he started on the good work: he did not even pause to take off his overcoat. He bestrode the patient, applied his mouth to hers, and thumped rhythmically on her bosom. Smoothly efficient though he and the nurse had been, the woman's cry and the commotion had wakened several of the other patients in adjacent beds. One of them sat bolt upright and took in the scene on the floor.

'Christ! Look at 'im, the dirty sod,' she yelled.

'Get yer 'ands off 'er,' shouted another, and two formidable-looking women leapt out of bed and rushed to the aid of their fellow patient. Despite his protests the anaesthetist was dragged off the victim and was only saved from further punishment by the arrival of the emergency team. It was his overcoat that was the cause of the trouble: if he'd been a painter and decorator wearing a white coat nobody would have interfered.

Perambulating surgeons are not very good at first aid, and we always hate unexpected attendance at the scenes of road accidents. We do not as a rule carry any of the necessary equipment and there is very little one can do to help. One night in the pouring rain my car broke down near Guildford and I invoked the aid of the A.A. depot just outside the city. A taxi was provided to take me home and I unwisely confided to the chatty driver that I was a doctor. One should never do this. After a few miles a police car swished past us at high speed with headlights ablaze.

'There's been an accident up front,' my driver announced with confident relish, and he was quite right. We soon came up on a queue of stationary vehicles and if I'd been on my own I would have skulked at the back of the queue. My driver had other ideas: he weaved his way to the front and proudly produced me, a real live doctor, at the focal point of the accident. And what an accident! There were cars all over the road, in the ditch and up the bank. The rain was coming down in torrents and lying in the middle of the road was the cause of the trouble ... a horse, which must have strayed into the traffic from an adjoining field. To my secret relief, the poor animal was dead. I can do little for humans in these circumstances and absolutely nothing for horses.

Miraculously, there was only one other casualty — a man sitting in the road with his eyes covered by a handkerchief which someone had tied round his head. The handkerchief was sodden with rain and blood, and I lifted it to have a look. There was a nasty gash on his forehead and I asked him to lie down. My driver looked at me expectantly and I eyed the knot of interested spectators. They were soaked to the skin but they weren't going to miss anything. I felt that the next move was up to me.

'Has anybody got a blanket or something to cover him with?'

Nobody moved. Resignedly I took off my own raincoat and spread it over the now prostrate form. Someone had sent for an ambulance and its authoritative siren could be heard approaching. It swept up, braked to a halt, and two uniformed men erupted from the opened doors. I stood back in deference to the experts and in a trice the casualty was on a stretcher, into the ambulance and away.

'Hell!' I said bitterly to my driver, 'I forgot to ask for my coat back.'

We drove to my home and comforted ourselves with a couple of large whiskies. That incident illustrates the general futility of Fellows of the Royal College of Surgeons trying to attend to roadside accidents. I have stopped a good number of times and usually announce my arrival by saying that I am a doctor. Nobody, in my experience, takes the slightest notice and there is always someone who knows more about first aid than I do.

'Don't move 'im,' they advise, or 'Mind 'is leg!'

Once, when I was examining a small boy who had been run over by a car, a woman tapped me on the shoulder.

'Would you have a look at my husband?' she said. 'He's got a bad heart and this has upset him.' I wasn't surprised that he was upset, because he turned out to be the chap who had run over the small boy.

When I was a student I was assigned to a very senior surgeon who was a Knight of the Realm. He was accustomed to taking a daily constitutional by walking from his home to the hospital, followed at a discreet interval by his chauffeur-driven Rolls Royce. There was much less traffic in those days. One morning he came up on the usual little crowd of bystanders gathered round a prostrate form. He was reluctantly aware of his duty and tried, with some difficulty, to get to the front.

'Excuse me,' he said quietly, 'I am a Professor of Surgery.'

The man who was bending over the casualty looked up. 'And I'm Jesus Christ.'

Quite often, as a statistical probability in the case of a road accident, there are one or two drunks about and they always want to be involved in whatever is going on. Their alcoholic euphoria leads them to take an optimistic view of the whole affair, regarding it as just another happening in a convivial evening.

Why, then, do we stop? Why don't we just pass by on the other side? I suppose it is because other people genuinely expect us to do something useful. I got a frightful telling off from my wife when I declined to do anything about a chap who was having an epileptic fit in the seat next to me in a London theatre – especially when he fell into the gangway. I was confident that someone would come and take him away, and I was keeping a surreptitious eye on his breathing, but I didn't hear the last of that for a long time. The other reason we stop is that we cherish the hope that one day we might really be of help and be able to stop someone bleeding or choking to death. This can happen, and it happened to a friend of mine, Michael Ball. He is a consultant general surgeon now, but he was our surgical registrar at the time and was driving with a friend to the hospital when he saw a car in the ditch. He stopped to investigate and found a man literally bleeding to death from a deep wound in his neck which had severed the jugular vein. Michael put his thumb on the wound, his friend drove the three miles to the hospital and Michael took the patient straight to the theatre, operated on him and gave him a blood transfusion. The patient left hospital in a few days, but he wasn't a local man and he didn't bother to thank Michael. He probably never knew how close he had been to death or appreciated the extraordinary chance that had saved him. He was probably worried about the car, and whether his insurance would pay for the damage.

I haven't seen Michael for many years but he was, and no doubt still is, a very interesting bloke. One day when we were having coffee in the surgeons' changing room he told me about a dinner party the evening before. He had the ill luck to sit next to a woman who was both patronising and ill-mannered.

'It's a pity,' she said, 'that you young doctors have no interests outside your work. It's all you can talk about.'

Michael, an accomplished mountaineer, was a little taken aback. He told her that he had just returned from an attempt on Mount Everest with Sir Edmund Hillary. It was the woman's turn to be taken aback:

'What did your mother have to say about that?'

Michael explained that his mother didn't really mind. She was another of these dull doctors: a busy G.P. most of the time, but at that moment she happened to be sailing her twenty-six footer across the Channel. In her spare time, he added, she writes detective stories, under the name of Josephine Bell.

Holidays abroad can be a fertile source of unexpected emergencies and opportunities for rendering, or avoiding, first aid. Thea and I have a great affection for France and its people and we go there nearly every year. We love the infinite variety and careless beauty of the countryside and the timeless dignity of the dilapidated villages and towns. The big cities are getting to look much like big cities everywhere else, but one can keep away from them. Many English tourists find French people aloof and stiff in their manner. I think this is because the French resent the English habit of coming abruptly, and to Gallic ears rudely, to the point. When we go into a shop in England we tend to ask for what we want without preamble. Most of us say please and thank you, but see no need for any further effusion. The French find this offensive: every transaction in their country starts with an appropriate greeting: *'Bonjour, M'sieu'* or *'Bon soir, Madame'* formally exchanged by both sides in the deal – and at the conclusion of the business, however trivial, there are equally polite if meaningless farewells. These routine courtesies cannot be translated into English because we have no equivalent and collective nouns for the sexes. Our use of Sir and Madam is a deferential one-way form of address quite unlike the companionable and classless French form. Once this difference in approach is understood, and the traditional courtesies observed, the French are found to be friendly, kind and generous, and they will go to any lengths to help someone in trouble. They are generous but they are also thrifty, and their thrift leads to some economies which we would do well to imitate. In France, windows open inwards. Ours open outwards and we have to employ an army of cleaners to keep them smart. The French buy their milk, along with the other hundred and one items needed for the kitchen, in a shop or supermarket. We have the stuff delivered, in amounts which are nearly always too much or too little, by a pleasant young man we hardly ever see, driving a uniquely appalling vehicle which was deliberately designed as a mobile traffic block. Like the rest of their continental neighbours the French are fiercely nationalistic, and if Edward Heath had understood this he would not have tried to sell them British Leyland trucks and cheddar cheese. This nationalism and an ostrich-like belief in their own infallibility make them peculiarly resistant to change, especially in the art of cooking, where they consider themselves, with some qualified justification, to be the best in the world. If only they could accept that other nations also eat food and may know a thing or two, their menus might become less stereotyped. The egg is a good example. French cooks do only two things with eggs: they boil them for ten minutes or they make them into omelettes. They have never learned to poach them, fry them, scramble them or stick them right side up in an eggcup — and they are jolly well not going to try. They serve hot food on cold plates, they mess about with butter and jam on the tablecloth instead of using sideplates, they eat strawberries without cream and they have never heard of marmalade, apple sauce with pork, grilled rashers of bacon, crumpets, buttered toast or roast beef and Yorkshire pudding. Their aperitifs are nauseating, and although they drink a fluid called 'Pschitt' with apparent relish, they are darned if they are going to drink Spanish sherry, English gin, German wine, a Portuguese digestif or a Scottish liqueur.

However, it is in the matter of lavatories that they are in a class of their own among civilized peoples. Their pride and joy is the hellish contrivance called a '*trou*' with which most travellers in their country are all too familiar. It consists of two oblong plates on which one is supposed to plant one's feet, on either side of a hole (the *trou*) for you know what. There is no toilet paper but with any luck there may be a fragmented copy of *Le Figaro*. There are no hooks on the door, and there may be no door. In recent years, as a concession to advancing world technology, a flush has been added. I have never discovered where the flush jets are located, but the deluge which results when the chain is pulled is obviously designed to cleanse the whole establishment, walls and all. The absence of a seat encourages one to adopt a primeval posture which is allegedly effort-effective, but it is not conducive to accurate aim and is more than likely to result in the loss of one's loose change and other valuables down the hole. I once lost my passport in this way and spent a very unpleasant ten minutes with my sleeve rolled up to the elbow trying to get it back.

My reason for going into this business in some detail is because I had a terrible experience in a ladies' lavatory in the vicinity of Limoges. Thea had, not to put too fine a point on it, been taken short — and when she is taken short there is a considerable element of urgency. Unfortunately her trouser zip was stuck at the top of its travel and her cries of distress demanded my attendance within. I wouldn't have minded if we had been the sole occupants of the premises, but I began my rescue operation by wrenching violently at the zip under the interested gaze of what appeared to be the Annual General Meeting of the Limoges Women's Institute. The zip more than made up in strength for its lack of efficiency and I was unable to tear it from its moorings. Only one course was open to me: a hundred yards sprint to where our car was parked, a frenzied search for a pair of scissors and a return sprint, encouraged as I neared the finish by anguished exhortations from Thea and the quiet approval of the ladies of Limoges. I just made it in time, otherwise this story would have had an even more dispiriting ending.

Cries for help come in many forms, and although I am a very poor swimmer I was once called upon to save a girl from drowning. To say that I am a poor swimmer errs on the side of flattery. I can do a sort of frog-like breast stroke which gets me very slowly from place to place provided the places are not too far apart. I can swim much better on my back but then I can't see where I'm going, and I always swim in a circle which gets me back to where I was in the beginning. Nobody who knows me, and who found themselves in peril of sinking into a watery grave, would apply to me for assistance; but the swimmer who turned to me in her time of need was a total stranger. It happened like this. My friend John Bishop and I were standing on the end of the jetty at a south coast seaside resort, watching the antics of a number of bathers disporting themselves on a raft which was moored about a hundred yards away.

John and I were hospital residents in Birmingham and were both training to be surgeons, but he had to abandon the idea a year or so later when he won the Military Cross and lost his left arm at one and the same moment during the Battle of El Alamein. He was Medical Officer to the 50th Royal Tank Regiment at the time and had decided that the best way to minister to his flock was to tour the battlefield in a scout car. This was his undoing, and set a bad example to his successors in the Regiment, one of whom was killed and the other awarded the DSO. I mention this to indicate that John was rather careless of his own safety, a fact which has some slight relevance to what followed. We were joined on the jetty by two small girls who looked as though they had the afternoon off from St Trinian's.

'Will you,' they said in unison, 'swim out to the raft with us?'

My instinct was to decline, but I had no time to put my views to John.

'Of course,' he said, and dived into the water with one of the little horrors. The remaining one gave me a trusting smile and did a belly flop into the deep. I cursed John silently and followed. Our performance, the little girl's and mine, was equally bad and we reached the raft together − but we couldn't get on to the damn thing. Far too many people were on it already and any addition tipped the raft to one side, when the newcomer fell off. This was a fairly tiring process, and after several fruitless attempts to clamber on board, my little girl − I never discovered her name − bobbed up from the depths.

'I'm drowning,' she said. 'Save me.'

I coughed up an ounce or so of seawater and asked, 'How old are you?'

'Ten,' she spluttered.

I grabbed a bit of the raft and looked her in the eye.

'If you wish to be eleven,' I said firmly, 'you will have to swim to the beach: it's no good trying to get back to the jetty.'

She stared at me in horrified disbelief, so I made the point quite clear. 'I'm drowning too.'

We set off in tandem and eventually arrived, quite exhausted, at the shore about 200 yards away. There was a gasping interlude during which neither of us moved. I didn't even think. She recovered first, got to her feet and gave me a look of such withering contempt that I can remember it to this day.

My last little story doesn't really come into the category of first aid, although that's the way it started. A middle-aged man who lived in another town came to the hospital to visit his friend Bill, who was a patient in one of the medical wards, but as he was walking past the gatekeeper's lodge he had a fit – and it is worth mentioning that he had never had a fit before and, as far as I know, never had one again. He was given first aid and was taken on a stretcher into the Casualty Department. The Casualty surgeon felt that his investigation would best be carried out in his home town, but deemed it wise to admit him overnight. He was put to bed but during the next few hours found himself unable to pass water: he had what we call acute retention of urine. The condition persisted in spite of a couple of hot baths, and when I was called to see him the following morning it was clear that he needed an immediate prostatectomy – removal of the prostate gland.

During my examination I found that he had severe haemorrhoids and that his straining to pass water had caused them to prolapse. His prostate operation was uneventful but the prolapsed and strangulated piles continued to give him a lot of trouble, so as soon as he was passing water normally I operated on him again and removed the piles. He made good progress after this and was looking forward to going home when fate struck this unlucky man another blow. He began to vomit blood and although he claimed that he had never suffered from indigestion, a barium X-ray showed a sizeable gastric ulcer. We gave him a blood transfusion but he continued to bleed quite severely and I therefore operated on him yet again, removing most of his stomach. A fortnight later he was ready for home, but although he was with us for several weeks I never saw that man smile. When I said goodbye he gave me a look which I thought contained a measure of resentment.

'All I wanted,' he said, 'was to see my friend Bill.'

PART TWO

WAR

Tunisia, Italy, the landings at Salerno, the final assaults on Cassino, and a bit more besides. This is not an account of the North African and Italian campaigns but of isolated incidents therein. It seems wrong that reminiscence should be constrained by time and place: in conversation it is never so. These things happened and it does not matter exactly when, or where or in what order.

Foreigners and Animals

A year or so back my son Nicolas was stopped by the police. He was wandering about Hammersmith in the middle of the night, shouting 'Yaaow' at the top of his voice and the police wanted to know why. My son explained that he was trying to find his cat, Yao. 'A little Burmese' he said. Had the police seen her? Nicolas and I share a love of animals – his love perhaps a little more eccentric than mine. As a child he was rarely without a mouse or two in his pockets, and in the cinema would bring them out to watch the film. He is more at home with rats, cats and mice than with horses, and his riding career has been eventful rather than distinguished but I think he would have been on my side in the matter of Private Luciano's horse ... except of course that it all happened before he was born.

At the time we were out of the line, just beyond the reach of the German guns, and resting in a little Italian village. We were resting, but there was no quiet. Our own gunners busied themselves with a methodical harassment of the enemy positions and occasionally there was the distant crump of a German reply. I was sitting on my bedroll in what had been a farm labourer's cottage. Nearly all the young people had left the village, but an old woman was still living in the squalid back room. She was dressed in the funereal black of the Italian peasant and the weathered brown of her lined and sorrowing face barely concealed the pallor of ill health. I spoke no Italian and did not know what had become of her family. About twice a day she would shuffle through my quarters with a muttered *'Buongiorno, Maggiore,'* and return an hour or so later with scraps of food. She seemed to live on vegetables, and sometimes we gave her a little meat and tinned milk from our rations. The village had been heavily shelled, and the dirt road was rutted by trucks, jeeps and screeching Bren-gun carriers. The vehicles were parked in haphazard fashion and all around was the exuberant bustle of military life: shouted orders and an occasional Rabelaisian pleasantry from some irrepressible Tommy. Often there was the sound of aircraft passing overhead: they were always ours and if their target was not too far away we could hear the detonation of their bombs. I shut my ears to the familiar sounds and tried to concentrate on Private Luciano's letter home. During quiet periods everyone wrote to their loved ones and it was among a pile of letters waiting to be censored. 'Our company commander,' he had written, 'is a right bastard.' I would have liked to know why Private Luciano thought I was a right bastard and I guessed that he had made the comment in his letter for the express purpose of bringing his considered opinion to my notice. He was, after all, entitled to say what he liked in a theoretically private correspondence provided there was no breach of security. Cunning little sod! I was still musing on his devious ways when he appeared in the doorway. He came more or less to attention and gave a grudging salute.

'I want to show you something,' he said, and I waited until he added a reluctant 'sir'.

In spite of his Italian surname, Private Luciano had been born in a Sussex village and in civilian life he was a groom. I think his Christian name was George, and if I had been a chestnut mare we would probably have got on very well. He was short, stocky and surly, and his dark looks proclaimed his Latin origin. I didn't know much about his antecedents, but his forebears had taken British nationality and with all the fanaticism of a convert Luciano hated foreigners. To tell the truth, he didn't seem to like anybody very much and in particular he didn't like me. So far as I knew I had never done him any harm and perhaps it was only that I was a symbol of the authority he detested. His hostility was confined to the human species and I knew from past experience that he loved animals, all animals. It was one of the reasons why I put up with his sullen insubordination. In Tunisia he had taken charge of a baby camel and bottle-fed it for weeks because its mother had been killed by a stray shell. One day it disappeared, and Luciano was not only inconsolable but deeply suspicious of his fellow squaddies. He was only partly mollified by the acquisition of a tiny piglet, also motherless and in need of his care and attention. I think the piglet must have had some glandular disorder because it never got any bigger. Luciano took it everywhere, and when we were within range of gunfire he dug a slit trench for it. Some of the soldiers said it had fleas and covered it with D.D.T. powder. It developed dermatitis as a result, and Luciano was furious. In the end it too disappeared, and this time I shared the suspicions he voiced about his comrades.

Because of all this, I had a feeling that his present request must have something to do with the animal kingdom. He didn't elaborate and as conversation with Luciano was never very rewarding I simply nodded my agreement, put down his letter and followed him through the rubble of the village. In a few minutes we came to the shattered remains of a small stone cottage, little more than a hovel. One miserable room was still standing and I had to stoop to get through the doorway. Inside was a horse! The room had one tiny window with jagged edges of broken glass and some light came from a hole in the roof. The animal was a big grey draught horse standing all of seventeen hands. It was trembling with fear, coated with mud and painfully thin, and when I drew near its ears went back and it flung its head up, almost touching the low ceiling. The frayed end of a rough headrope showed where it had broken away from its tether. An old wooden chair was lying in one corner of the room but there was no other furniture. The stone floor was covered with droppings and urine and the place stank of ammonia.

'He's bomb-happy,' said Luciano. The horse, I noticed, was a 'he' not an 'it'.

'How on earth did it get in here?' I asked.

'I dunno. 'E must 'ave put 'is 'ead down and barged into the room in a panic.' Luciano pointed to a raw fly-infested wound where its withers had struck the lintel.

'Can you get him out?'

'No,' said Luciano. 'No amount of pulling or pushing would get 'im through that door now.' He paused and there was a curious expression on his face, a mixture of pleading and defiance. He turned away and said almost casually, 'I'll look after 'im, if you like.'

Luciano couldn't bear to ask a favour from me but I could sense his desperation. I inspected the room more closely. Hovel it may have been, but the walls were of stone and over a foot thick. I made a mental note to ask the Engineers to demolish a wall and set the animal free, but they were busy and I doubted if they would give Luciano's horse a very high priority. Besides, an assault on the wall with sledgehammers would terrify the unfortunate beast. Explosives were out of the question, and if we disturbed the lintel the remains of the roof would almost certainly come down. So I decided to let matters rest.

'You look after it, Luciano,' I said and turned on my heel.

As the weeks went by the horse put on weight, its wound healed and its coat began to gleam from twice daily grooming. Its flowing mane and tail were lovingly combed and its feathered fetlocks shone proudly white above oiled and polished hooves. The floor was clean and smelt vaguely of disinfectant, and Luciano had found some bales of straw to make a bed. I suspect that he filched some oats from the cookhouse every day, and there were other sources of fodder within reach. Accommodation in this part of the world was strictly limited and some of my men had found curious billets. Two of them shared a cowshed with a surprisingly docile bull and another pair made a very comfortable dwelling by excavating a sizeable hole in a haystack. The excavated hay was appropriated for the horse and when it ran short the stack-dwellers willingly provided more by making their home a bit larger. Luciano scoured the area for anything the horse would eat and occasionally he found, or stole, an apple or a turnip. He mellowed, and no longer fixed me with a baleful eye whenever we met. Even the NCOs took a sympathetic view of the enterprise and Luciano seemed to be relieved of most of his military duties. Indeed, 'the stables', as he now referred to the hovel which he shared with his friend, was never short of visitors and little titbits were produced from the pockets of soldiers lounging in for a gossip. Luciano had never been so popular.

This idyll could not last, and the time came when we were ordered to move. I was busy all that day in the truck which served as a company office, but when I got back to my billet Private Luciano was waiting for me. He did not salute but I was so struck by his dejected appearance that I forgot to tick him off.

'I've got to shoot 'im,' he said.

I was in no doubt that 'im was the horse.

'What on earth for?'

It seemed that Luciano had heard on the grapevine that we were to be relieved by a Polish unit. Nobody had told me, but that wasn't surprising.

'So what?' I said.

'Foreigners!' said Luciano disgustedly. 'They won't treat 'im right.'

I argued in vain. Luciano was adamant: he was not going to leave his friend to the mercy of a bunch of foreigners. It would have to be destroyed, and in the end I deferred to his superior knowledge.

The next morning, when I had finalized the orders for our departure, I walked through the village to pay my last respects to the horse. I found Luciano sitting on his rickety chair, scribbling on a piece of paper. His friend was munching hay and turned his soft gaze on me when I came through the doorway. I ran a hand down his glossy neck and rubbed his head between the ears. Luciano looked up, and to my surprise he was beaming.

'It's all right, sir,' he said. 'It's not the Poles; it's the New Zealanders.'

'Does that make a difference?'

'Of course it does. New Zealanders ain't foreigners, not really.'

He handed me the piece of paper and I saw that it was a crude map, giving six figure references for all sources of fodder in the vicinity.

'Will you please give this map to the New Zealand C.O., sir.'

It was an order, and I nodded gravely. I was pleased that Luciano had decided not to shoot our trusting old friend, but privately I thought there might be some flaws in his xenophobic logic. I had heard that the Poles were fine cavalrymen and maybe they were a nation of horse lovers, whereas any New Zealanders I had met seemed to have a very pragmatic approach to livestock and were more concerned with an animal's value than with its feelings. However, I'd had enough of arguing with Private Luciano and I accepted his decision.

That afternoon the trucks, jeeps and ambulances rolled out and the village echoed to the sound of revving engines and shifting gears. Some of the transport had been left behind at our rear headquarters and there was a sizeable body of marching troops following in the dust of the trucks. Luciano was among them, but I looked away as he passed: I didn't want to see the desolation in his eyes. Three weeks later we were moved again. It was army policy to keep us constantly on the move. It must have cost a fortune in fuel but it was supposed to keep us alert and busy with the special problems of each new area. As soon as we had settled in, Luciano came to see me. I knew what he wanted.

'All right,' I said, 'we'll go and have a look.'

I took a jeep and we set off to find the village. The New Zealanders were still there, and by rights I should have paid a courtesy call on their commanding officer. I didn't, because I was a little hesitant about explaining my reason for this visitation. When I had given him Luciano's map he had laughed and tossed it aside. We parked the jeep and made our way to the familiar hovel. Luciano, almost running, was ahead of me and called out, 'There's the stables.' I caught up with him in the doorway. Four soldiers were in the room, playing vingt-et-un, and the floor was littered with their equipment. One of them was sitting on an upturned bucket, the bucket which Luciano had used to water the horse. Two were sitting on bales of straw and the last was on the chair with his back to me. I saw that he had a lance-corporal's stripe. He looked over his shoulder, then glanced back at his cards.

'I'll stick,' he said, and got to his feet. He looked at me enquiringly: 'Sir?'

I began rather awkwardly, 'There used to be a horse ...'

Luciano interrupted belligerently, 'Wot's 'appened to 'im?'

The man on the bucket stubbed out his cigarette. 'The Eyeties took him.'

'How?' said Luciano. 'No one could 'ave got 'im through that door.'

The soldier pointed to a rifle leaning against the wall and touched his forehead between the eyes.

He grinned. 'Don't worry, chum. We got him out.'

I make no apology for lumping foreigners and animals together in the title of this chapter because it seems to me that our attitude to foreigners is often conditioned by their behaviour towards the animal kingdom. We tend to associate each nationality with a particular species, always with opprobrium and usually with total disregard for our own bad habits. We know that Spaniards enjoy bullfights and Filipinos love cockfights, that the French eat frogs and horses, the Chinese eat dogs and the Corsicans eat blackbirds, that the Japanese slaughter too many whales and the Canadians slaughter too many baby seals, that the North Americans exterminated the buffalo and the Australians tried to exterminate the bunny rabbit. They all do things which we would not do, or do not do any longer, or are not allowed to do. We find lovable the creatures that other peoples are beastly to, and we try not to remember our own intensive farms, our experimental laboratories, the bewildered dogs abandoned on our highways, our foxes and deer, our badgers and otters.

I formed a lasting hatred for all Arabs after my enforced sojourn in Algeria and Tunisia because of their diabolical treatment of that patient, long-suffering and delicately beautiful little beast, the donkey. It is fitting that the donkey wears the sign of the Cross upon its back and I have seen these poor little animals beaten with chains, kicked in the stomach, and frequently loaded beyond endurance. Some of my men who found an Arab thrashing his tiny donkey made the man pick it up and flogged him along the road with his own whip. This helped to relieve their feelings but no doubt the Arab took his revenge on the unfortunate little beast later on. My son, who knows far more about Arabs than I do, tells me that the Bedouin can be very devoted to their camels. He ought to know, for he has lived with the Bedu for many months at a time, but I witnessed another scene in Tunisia which roused me and the few soldiers who were with me, at first to fury and then to violent intervention. A burly French farmer was having an altercation with a ragged follower of the Prophet whom he accused of stealing a load of wood from the farm. The wood was piled high on a donkey's back and the Arab encouraged it to keep going by whacking its slender rump with a thick stick. Every time he did this the Frenchman brought the animal to a trembling halt by punching it savagely in the face. I expect the Arab had indeed stolen the wood and he certainly needed it more than the Frenchman, but our sympathies were with neither protagonist — only with the donkey who was being subjected to such vicious and undeserved punishment. We solved the immediate problem with Solomon-like impartiality: we off-loaded the donkey, confiscated the Arab's stick and sent him on his way with a valedictory kick up the backside, and left the Frenchman to collect his miserable heap of wood from the roadside. On another occasion I was being driven through Constantine in a staff car when we came to a steep hill. In front of us an emaciated horse was struggling to pull a large overburdened cart up the slope. Its unshod hooves were slipping on the cobbled surface and an Arab, still standing on the cart, was lashing it with a long whip. I stopped the car and my driver and I set our shoulders to the back of the cart. The whip continued to whistle through the air and I half expected to feel its lash on my own back. My driver, a normally cheerful young man from Staffordshire by the name of Charlie Beddows, was in angry mood. He was noted for his colourful but rather repetitive vocabulary.

'If that fucking whip touches me,' he said, 'I'll fucking well kill the bugger.'

I was never able to work up any great hatred against the German army, for the Wehrmacht who fought against us in North Africa and Italy were brave and chivalrous soldiers, and when they finally surrendered in Tunisia we were not surprised to find that they had a sizeable quota of canine camp followers. Regrettably, and with many sad farewells, these animals had to be handed over. In one hastily improvised P.O.W. cage the Germans were drawn up on parade and the dog owners among them stepped forward one by one to hand their pets over to the British guards, a detachment of Sherwood Foresters. The dogs were mostly Alsatians or big mongrels, but a roar of laughter went up from both Germans and British when a very tall and very thin Kraut officer led out, on an immensely long lead, a tiny dog about the size of a Mexican Chihuahua. Perhaps I should be reproved for calling a German officer a Kraut, but the appellation merits a little thought. The tabloid press was apt, in time of war, to refer to the enemy as the Hun or the Boche. So far as I know, soldiers never used these pejorative terms. In World War I in the trenches, the grey-uniformed chap floundering about in the mud on the other side of no-man's-land was known, almost affectionately, as Fritz or Jerry. In Italy we always called the enemy Krauts and I think that this nickname, loosely translated as 'me old cabbage', implied not only the innate comradeship of one soldier for another, but also the deep conviction of our troops that they were superior to their enemy – as indeed they proved to be.

We too moved round with a small menagerie of four-legged friends: dogs, mules, and of course, Luciano's camel and his pig. The American army did not seem to have any quadruped component, which was a little surprising because if anyone is indelibly linked by phrase and fable to an animal species it is the North American to his horse. I fear that relations between the two may have become a bit strained over the years. Stories of the way in which cowboy bronco-busters tamed and broke wild horses for a dollar a time do not make pleasant reading, and however much one may admire the spirit of young men who try to ride a bucking bronco at a rodeo, one's admiration is tempered by knowledge of the fiendish means which are used to make the bronco buck: the rope or strap which is cruelly tightened round the animal's flanks to inflict excruciating pressure on its genitalia. I used to be fond of watching 'Western' films but I have become sickened by the way in which countless unsuspecting horses are brought crashing to the ground by hauling simultaneously on the cruel western bit and on a cord attached to one or other foreleg, and I am suspicious of the speed with which the camera always swings away from the stricken animal.

However, my experience of American fighting men, the non-equestrian variety, was highlighted by a memorable weekend when the brigade to which we were attached, the 1st Guards Brigade, took over from an American combat team in the Apennines, a combat team being the evocatively named equivalent of a British brigade. Our Brigade Commander, a tall ebullient aristocrat, seemed for some undisclosed reason to have a pretty hearty dislike of the entire American nation and his normally impeccable good manners left a good deal to be desired in his dealings with our transatlantic allies. He decided that before we took over the position, which was seven or eight miles off the beaten track in difficult mountainous terrain, we would carry out a reconnaissance. The reconnaissance party consisted of himself and his Brigade Major and Staff Captain, the three Battalion Commanders and their seconds-in-command, the Lieutenant-Colonel commanding the brigade artillery, the Lieutenant-Colonel commanding the Royal Engineers, and myself. I commanded No. 1 Field Ambulance and was accompanied by two of my officers, Major Field and Captain Fletcher. We set off at high speed in our seven jeeps, the Brigadier's leading and ours bringing up the rear. It was a feature of this part of the front that north of a certain line the main roads to the American and British sectors were quite separate. There was a British road and an American road, and where theirs began the Americans had established a checkpoint. As we neared their sector a huge notice board warned us that the checkpoint lay ahead and that we would be required to stop and state our business. The Brigadier knew, and from past experience his Battalion Commanders knew, that there was no way he was going to stop, anywhere, any time, for any bloody American. I did not know this, and nor did the Americans. When our convoy of jeeps approached the checkpoint a white-helmeted sergeant of military police strolled into the middle of the road and raised a confident and authoritative hand to bring us to a halt. The Brigadier's driver accelerated to about sixty m.p.h. and the startled American dived for safety. The Battalion Commanders were close behind and were through before the infuriated man had scrambled to his feet. The gunners and sappers just made it, but, taken unawares, we still had fifty yards to go. By this time the checkpoint was a hive of activity: a dozen American G.I.s were leaping up and down and some of them were reaching for their weapons. They began to push a barrier across the road but our grinning driver was equal to the challenge: his foot was flat on the accelerator and we hurtled into the ever-narrowing gap. The offside of the jeep struck the end of the barrier and sent it flying. We were through! We looked back at the pandemonium behind us, then raced after the rest of our convoy. As we got further north the road was crammed with American transport, jeeps and four-wheel-drive trucks. Anywhere off the road was a foot deep in mud. The Brigadier's jeep continued flat out and, British style, on the left of the road, its horn blowing continuously. We all tucked in close behind and after a rather hairy drive we reached the point where we left the main road and began to climb along muddy tracks into the mountains. We found the headquarters of the combat team established in tents in a little hollow and the Brigadier was introduced to the American General. I cannot pretend that this meeting of minds did much for Anglo-American accord, and the General, a rather elderly man with steely blue eyes behind horn-rimmed spectacles, seemed a bit vague about the exact disposition of his troops.

'I guess we got a coupla squads about here,' he said, prodding uncertainly at the operations map pinned to a blackboard. However, he was courteous and hospitable, and after concentrating for a few minutes on where some more of his squads might be, he offered us lunch.

'No thank you,' said the Brigadier ungraciously. 'We have our own rations.'

This was quite untrue; we had nothing. The discussion about the handover went on for another half-hour or so, and then a young American lieutenant, who seemed to be the messing officer, lost patience. He wanted his lunch even if the Brigadier did not. He grabbed the Brigadier's sleeve.

'C'mon, bud,' he said. 'Let's eat.'

I waited for the explosion, but the Brigadier was no fool; he knew when he was beaten. He turned to the lieutenant with a charming smile. 'Thank you so much,' he said. 'We'd be delighted.'

It was a splendid lunch and the unfamiliar American rations made a very pleasant change. The pudding was a jam roly-poly and I had a second helping.

After the meal we set off on foot into the hills to make contact with our opposite numbers and to reconnoitre the lie of the land. My main objective was to find the regimental aid post of the American battalion in the line. This would be the point at which my stretcher bearers would assume responsibility for the evacuation of casualties over what was obviously going to be a long and arduous route. As we got near, the position of the aid post was all too apparent — to us and no doubt to the enemy. I asked Major Field and Captain Fletcher to look around for a better site and went on up to the post. It was in a building, a house of sorts, with immensely thick stone walls but little in the way of a roof. It was almost on the skyline and its upper part must have been in full view of the Krauts. A cow, with its entrails hanging out of a ghastly wound in its belly, was lying near the entrance. As I passed it made a feeble movement with its head, but the urgent whistle of an incoming mortar bomb made me duck hastily into the building. A badly wounded soldier was lying on a stretcher on the floor. His face was ashen and a blanket covered a roughly splinted leg. One of his comrades, with a bloodstained bandage round his head, was squatting beside him. A number of G.I.s wearing Red Cross brassards were lounging about, smoking and talking, and watching a harassed-looking medical officer and an orderly trying to set up a plasma drip on a soldier who was lying on another stretcher supported by trestles. I told the officer who I was, but he was understandably preoccupied and when I ventured to suggest that he might be better off if he were a little further down the hill he looked at me uncomprehendingly. He told me that the battalion was taking heavy casualties and I asked how he evacuated them. I asked because we had been puzzled by the absence of stretcher-bearer posts on the way up. He gave me a brief outline of his method ... a method so bizarre that it was almost unbelievable. Another mortar bomb exploded outside and I felt it was time to leave; I had seen and heard enough. Outside, the cow was still. Its head had dropped into the dirt and its dry lolling tongue and glazed eyes showed that its ordeal was over.

'Toffee' Field and Fletcher were sitting on a boulder, waiting for me. They had found a good place, in dead ground and with a rudimentary building, for the Guards' Medical Officer to set up shop when he arrived. We talked for a while, discussing the problems of the takeover, and they were appalled when I described the American evacuation plan. It seemed that a sizeable posse of stretcher-bearers was retained in the exposed aid post at the top of the hill. These were the chaps I'd seen lounging about, and I understood there were more in another part of the building. When a number of casualties were ready to go down the whole posse set off, taking turn about at carrying the stretchers. As soon as they had departed, a radio message was sent to the combat team H.Q., and a relieving posse was despatched on the seven-mile uphill trek – the two groups crossing half-way. We started on our return journey and after about an hour we met the upward-bound American posse carrying a couple of stretchers. The casualties I'd seen in the aid post were evidently on their way down. What an extraordinary arrangement!

In less than an hour we were back at the combat team headquarters. The steely-eyed General was standing, arms folded, in front of his operations map. He looked none too pleased and the Brigadier was as usual speaking his mind. He was brusquely deploring the number of American casualties. Strictly speaking this was none of his business, but I shall never forget the General's chilling reply.

'There's plenty more,' he said, 'where they came from.'

The Brigadier left without another word and we drove off in our jeeps, jolting and slithering down the narrow track to the main road. This time my jeep was leading and we got hopelessly stuck in a patch of deep mud. The brigade jeep was immediately behind me and there was no room to pass. The Brigadier had had a trying day; this must surely be the last straw and we waited for his wrath to descend. We were saved by a diverting little incident which relieved the tension all round. It brought a wan smile to the Brigadier's face and was pure joy for the rest of us. A bareheaded gum-chewing American G.I., his hands in his pockets and a cigarette drooping from the side of his mouth, had seen our predicament. He wandered over to the Brigadier's jeep and stared at its furious occupant. I don't think he could have seen a high-ranking British officer before and he bent down to peer intently at the insignia on the Brigadier's shoulder. Then he straightened up, took the cigarette out of his mouth and shouted to a figure in the distance.

'Lootenant,' he bawled, 'this guy's a three-star general.'

If I have seemed to imply that our gallant allies were a touch incompetent, I am being unfair. Perhaps they weren't all that hot on mountain warfare. Perhaps they had never been in the mountains before. They would learn, as we had done, and they were immensely helpful to us over the next few days. For a start the 'lootenant' winched my jeep out of the mud. American vehicles, unlike our Bedfords, could winch anything out of anything. In the meantime we had one hell of a problem. In two days' time the

Guards would be marching into these hills. We had to provide a Main Dressing Station with a Field Surgical Unit attached, on or near the main road and link it to the Guards' regimental aid post by a seven-mile-long stretcher-bearer chain — and we had forty-eight hours in which to do it. We would be a tiny British enclave in American-held territory, and every building along the main road was filled to the brim with Yanks. Their four-wheel-drive trucks were floundering about quite happily in the sea of mud to either side of the road, but none of our two-wheel-drive Bedfords would dare set a wheel in the all-pervading goo.

I could find a hundred stretcher-bearers from our own resources but we needed three hundred. Our problem, reduced to its essentials, was this: I had to have, and quickly, two hundred extra stretcher bearers, a large building and hard standing for forty vehicles.

I began by enlisting the aid of the Brigade Staff Captain, Dicky Paget-Cooke. He was a charming, persuasive chap and we plodded through the mud to beard the American Divisional Commander in his frenetic headquarters. We explained our difficulty and he was amazingly sympathetic. Without further ado he scribbled on a piece of paper and handed it to me. That flimsy little chit was worth very much more than its weight in gold. It gave me authority to evict an American anti-tank regiment from their snug quarters on the main road. Jesus! We couldn't believe our luck. The building had everything we needed, and to our astonishment the anti-tank C.O. did not demur. He got out. What wonderful chaps these Americans were! We were in the nick of time: our lorries, thirty of them, were on the move. Already they had passed through the famous checkpoint and were crawling up the crowded American road towards us. Now for the stretcher-bearers. Dicky said he could 'borrow' some dismounted Yeomanry and they duly arrived — splendid chaps, and quite glad to have something to do. Finally I appealed to the D.D.M.S., the senior medical officer in the British Corps. He was a strange extrovert little man, but he turned up trumps — with a detachment of Italian soldiery conjured out of nowhere and about 150 strong. Their officers were smart enough but the men were a pretty disconsolate lot. They were festooned with cooking pots and pans, but several of them had no boots and one had no trousers. We made up their deficiencies in clothing, and in the event they proved to be superb stretcher-bearers, willing, tireless and uncomplaining. Unlike the British, they always carried the loaded stretchers shoulder high. Someone said, unkindly and unjustly, that they looked like waiters. We had a bit of trouble with their officers, whose relationship with their men was rather less democratic than our own, and who seemed to think that their soldier servants should carry their masters' belongings. We made it clear to them in no uncertain manner that this feudal approach conflicted with our method of establishing a long stretcher carry in mountainous terrain. This was to send the personnel up first, officers, NCOs and men disposing themselves in groups of four at intervals of about 200 yards, our boys first, then the dismounted Yeomanry, then the Italians. The eventual human chain was about seven miles long and once the men were on the ground, supplies of all kinds — blankets, bivouac tents, stretchers and rations — could be ferried up and casualties brought down with surprising rapidity. The chain could also be used by the battalion. By the third day everything and everyone was in place — the 3rd Bn, Welsh Guards, their regimental aid post with Captain Dai Morris, MC, in charge, the stretcher-bearer link, the main dressing station and field hospital. We all felt rather pleased with ourselves, and up front, in what was a holding sector, the Guards had no intention of taking heavy casualties. Their collective experience and discipline played a part in this, and so did the private enterprise of their Commanding Officer. He was an excessively good-looking and charismatic eccentric who roved tirelessly round his mountain domain carrying an American carbine. His immediate ambition was to ensure that the men under his command remained invisible, both to the enemy and to him. If he saw anyone, friend or foe, he was liable to shoot at them.

This was not our only contact with the Americans, but it was, I think, the most illuminating; and as so often an animal was unwittingly involved. The dying cow was both a victim and a symbol of the misery which warring humans have brought and will always bring to creatures which have never done them harm. The Americans were friendly, hospitable, casual and mightily helpful. What would Private Luciano, left behind in my old unit, have thought of them, of these English-speaking strangers who shed their blood so freely in the common cause, yet left a cow slowly and miserably to die when a single bullet could have brought it peace? Foreigners? ... or not really.

Water Obstacles

Now, who be ye would cross Lochgyle,
This dark and stormy water?

Thomas Campbell
Lord Ullin's Daughter.

A few years ago Thea and I spent an idyllic week in France with our friends John and Susan, cruising the Canal du Midi in a rather smart river boat which we had hired from the boatyard at Castelnaudary. The weather was perfect and our passage through each lock was, for us, quite an event. The *éclusiers*, the lock-keepers, or sometimes their wives, would wind away at a lock gate while one of us did the same on the opposite side. John, who lost an arm at El Alamein, soon made a name for himself as the fastest one-armed lock-gate winder the locals had ever seen. We bought eggs, fruit and vegetables from the *éclusiers* for lunch, fed sweets to the children and biscuits to the dogs, and in the evenings we tied up and walked a mile or so to the nearest restaurant. One cannot imagine a more peaceful scene or a more agreeable way of spending one's time.

One evening I fell to musing on the strange and often violent events I had heard about or witnessed in connection with canals and rivers, and the means for crossing them. Waterways have played an important part in almost every aspect of our social, military and economic history but the soldier takes such a limited professional view of their function that he lumps them all together under the heading 'water obstacles'. That is what water means to him — something which gets in his way and has to be crossed or something that may get in the way of, and deny ground to, an enemy. Put water and soldiers together and there's bound to be trouble. In another chapter I have written about the River Rapido at Cassino, of how it was crossed in little boats or by swimmers, and of the terrible and bloody toll it exacted from those who essayed the crossing, but there were many incidents where there was humour as well as trouble.

One of my colleagues in the medical services of the 46th Division was a Major 'O', universally known as Olly — a charming and very industrious and innovative officer but he had two attributes which are of some relevance to what follows: he was rather short-sighted and he was an inveterate chatterbox. The bit of the British army that he happened to be interested in at the time was withdrawing across a river and Olly, conscientious man that he was, went down to the river bank to make sure that no wounded had been left behind. He conferred with a trio of rather lugubrious Sherwood Foresters who were manning a little boat. They assured him that the far bank was populated entirely by Herrenvolk and that no further enquiry was indicated. However, Olly was not to be put off so easily and he required them to row him across the river. Once there, he clambered up the bank and disappeared from view. The Sherwood Foresters hastily withdrew. Their advice proved to have been sound, for Olly had not gone very far before he was apprehended by a couple of Krauts and marched off to the local Wehrmacht headquarters. There he was questioned at some length and his German interrogators were subjected to the full impact of Olly's personality. Not only was he a non-stop talker but he was also fluent in German. After about two hours they had had enough, and the officer in charge detailed an *obergefreiter* (corporal) to put Olly in a *kubelwagen* and return him, for God's sake, to the British lines. The *kubelwagen* set off in the general direction of the river, but the *obergefreiter* did not share his officer's chivalrous attitude to Olly's immediate future. Unaware that his prisoner spoke German he discussed with the driver of the vehicle several methods, all of them violent and lethal, by which they might dispose of their unwanted passenger. Olly was not the man to acquiesce in his own murder without saying a few words in mitigation and self-defence, and he was just about to speak up when fate intervened from above. A British fighter streaked low over the trees, spotted the *kubelwagen* and opened up with its cannon. The *kubelwagen* screeched to a halt, the driver and the *obergefreiter* flung themselves out of the car, and Olly leaped over the other side. He may have been a chatterbox but he was an astute and determined man and he lit out for home, sprinting flat out for the river. His glasses had fallen off in the commotion but he could just discern a bridge in front of him. He was still going like the clappers when he reached the middle, but alas, the far side of the bridge had been blown, and short-sighted Olly hurtled into the water. A short swim brought him home and wet, with even more to chatter about than usual.

There are many ways of crossing a water obstacle, but one particular method can be used when the water is at the bottom of a deep ravine. A steel cable is stretched across the gap and anchored by stakes driven into the ground some distance from the cliff edge. The cable is then made bar taut by wedging wooden shears — two wooden beams bolted together near one end — between the ground and the cable. A trolley of some kind is slung from the cable by pulleys and drawn from one side of the ravine to the other by ropes. We used this device twice, once in training and once for real. Both occasions were memorable and had some features in common. The first was a rather amateurish affair constructed by my own unit, using barrage balloon cable, and the trolley was a simple stretcher for carrying one wounded man. It seemed to work well in practice and we had no hesitation in offering to demonstrate our contrivance when the unit was inspected by General Montgomery. We did not happen to have a ravine handy, so we chose a small pond which we thought would serve for the purpose of the demonstration. The apparatus was rigged and ready when the great man arrived, and a volunteer 'casualty' was firmly strapped to the stretcher.

'All right,' said Monty. 'Let's see how it works.'

The rope party on the other side of the pond hauled away with a will, and the casualty sped rapidly down the sagging cable. Just as he reached the middle of the pond the shears on our side collapsed and the unfortunate soldier, still strapped to his stretcher, disappeared into the depths. There was a frantic rescue drama as fully clad swimmers launched themselves into the pond from both sides. Monty watched just long enough to see the furiously vocal volunteer safe and sound, then he turned to me.

'What would you do,' he said, 'for a wounded man in great pain, trapped inside a tank?'

I must confess that, as we were with an infantry division and hadn't got any tanks, I had never pondered this particular problem, but I said that I would give the poor chap an injection of tubunic morphine.

'What's that?' said Monty.

I produced one of the ingenious little tubunic syringes which are rather like a tiny toothpaste tube with a needle attached. Monty had never seen one before and he was quite interested. He examined the device and cast a reflective eye on his accompanying aides. I think he was toying with the idea of using one of them for a practical demonstration, but after a moment he gave me a satisfied nod and moved on.

The second occasion, for real, was in Italy and the ravine was wide and fearsomely deep. The construction, this time, was in the experienced hands of the Royal Engineers and was altogether more impressive. The cable was at least four times the diameter of our balloon cable and the trolley was very heavy and capable of carrying several men, but the principle of the apparatus was exactly the same. The Royal Engineers have a tradition that they always test any potentially dangerous contrivance with their own men before allowing other arms of the service to use it. I was glad of that. I watched the final stages of the erection with great interest, and in due course the officer in charge detailed two sapper 'volunteers' to get into the trolley. A rope party of twenty men was assembled on the far side of the ravine and as they pulled the trolley away it sank deeper and deeper into the void as its great weight stretched the cable. Suddenly the same misfortune befell the professional set-up as had happened to our amateur effort. The shears gave way and the trolley with its occupants plunged into the abyss. Fortunately the cable, and the mighty stakes driven into the ground, held firm – and the trolley, after several monumental bounces, came to rest at the apex of the taut 'V' of cable. The white-faced sapper volunteers looked anxiously upward at their tormentors, and a reinforced rope party hauled them laboriously up the steeply sloping cable on the far side. Stronger shears were made up and wedged more firmly than before, and another pair of reluctant heroes was launched into space. This time all was well and the cable trolley was used for troops, stores and casualties for many weeks. I never really liked using the infernal contraption because the trolley would sway and creak horribly as the rope parties hauled away with great concerted heaves, and on every trip I half-expected that the shears would give way again, but they never did.

Just before I wrote this I was watching television images of our troops wading ashore into the icy waters of the South Atlantic at Fitzroy in the Falkland Islands. Fate, and the Argentinian air force, struck a cruel blow to the men of the task force and to the Welsh Guards in particular, in that dreadful place. My thoughts are with them, and with the memory of an older battalion of the same Regiment. It was in the winter of 1944 and the 3rd Bn, Welsh Guards was taking up a position on some forgotten mountain in the Apennines. The weather was bitterly cold and we had to cross a mountain stream swollen to a torrent by rain and snow. We waded waist-high in the icy water, the soldiers raising their weapons above their heads with one hand and steadying themselves against the fierce rush of the water by holding on to a rope which had been stretched from one bank to the other. It was dusk by the time the last of the men had crossed, and in the morning they were almost frozen from the waist down. Dry blankets were supposed to be coming up on mules, and would somehow have been ferried across the stream, but in the darkness the muleteers lost their way and some of the animals plunged over a cliff into a ravine. This episode was followed by a small epidemic of the unpleasant and incapacitating condition known as trench foot, from which our soldiers suffered so severely in the First World War and again in the Falklands. The brigade commander sent me a message asking how this could be avoided in the future. I replied with a short report pointing out that the predisposing factors were cold and wet, and that the problem was logistic, not medical. Dry boots and dry socks were the only answer. In 1944 our soaking wet and freezing guardsmen were not immortalized on television, but millions of viewers saw the burned and wounded survivors coming ashore at Fitzroy against the terrible backcloth of the blazing *Sir Galahad*. One soldier typified the indomitable and irrepressible spirit of the British Tommy. He grinned at the cameraman as he stumbled out of the water.

'If I'd wanted to paddle,' he said, 'I'd have gone to Blackpool.'

Such men are very difficult to defeat.

My fear of heights has caused me a lot of embarrassment over the years, but on one occasion my predicament was shared with another of like mind, with Dai, the Medical Officer of that same battalion of the Welsh Guards. He and I were returning to our respective headquarters and we knew that we would have to negotiate a very deep ravine which lay across our path. The huge bridge which was the normal method of crossing had been demolished by the retreating Germans, but our engineers were in the process of constructing a replacement Bailey bridge. Eventually it became quite famous as the longest Bailey bridge ever to be erected in Italy, and at each end there was a large sign proclaiming it to be ASAMFU Bridge. Anyone who enquired into the origin of this curious name was told that the letters stood for 'A Self-Adjusting Military Fuck Up'. It was made by pushing great lengths of steel framework from each side of the ravine until they met in the middle. This process was under way, but the two elements had not yet met up with each other and there was an obvious gap about four feet wide in the middle. There was no floor to the bridge at this stage; it was just a great steel skeleton. After one horrified look, Dai, whose dislike of heights was about the same as mine, agreed wholeheartedly with my suggestion that we use the diversion, a path about half a mile long which had been cleared down the side of the ravine, across, and up the other side. Unfortunately we were not alone; we were accompanied by another officer, Lieutenant Peter Wills of the 3rd Bn, Grenadier Guards, who was made of sterner stuff.

'It's much quicker across the bridge,' he said, and started to climb on to the skeleton. Unwilling at this stage to appear too craven, we followed him, though very reluctantly. We clambered, it seemed endlessly, along those damned girders until we got to the middle. The two ends of the bridge were swaying slightly in the wind and the gap, which now looked longer than four feet, was spanned by a single warped plank less than a foot wide. The drop into the ravine was horrific and I could see the rocks and a trickle of water far below. I felt physically sick. Peter did not hesitate for a moment, he just walked across the plank − which wobbled under his feet. I looked at Dai and was glad to see that he had turned a sort of ashen colour.

'Can you do it?' I said.

'No, boyo, I bloody well can't.'

'And nor,' I said shakily, 'can I.'

A couple of sappers, standing on the girders on the far side and grinning all over their faces, were in splendid form.

'Come on,' they yelled. 'We haven't lost anyone yet.'

I don't think I have ever disliked anyone as much as those two excellent young men; except possibly Peter Wills, who was now disappearing into the distance. I would like to say that we overcame our fear and walked that beastly plank, but we didn't. We went all the way back along the girders and round the diversion. In case Dai happens to read this (he's a consultant surgeon now) I'd better mention that some time after this awful humiliation he was awarded the MC and was twice Mentioned in Despatches.

ASAMFU Bridge was notorious for another incident, a horrible and unforgettable one. An Italian girl was caught nearby under circumstances which suggested that she was an enemy spy and she was brought to the headquarters of a battalion which must of necessity be nameless. The commanding officer questioned her, and after a short 'trial' ordered that she be executed on the spot. The soldiers who were given this dreadful order, and the medical officer who was required to witness the shooting, were shocked and deeply ashamed.

At about the time when Olly was making his dash for freedom there had been a spate of rather similar incidents in which captured British stretcher-bearers had been returned to their own lines by the Germans. This courtesy was not reciprocated by the British, mainly because the Allied High Command feared a repetition of the famous Christmas fraternization which had occurred in the Flanders trenches in 1914. On 19 October, 1943, a German officer waving a white flag, and followed by an orderly carrying a bottle of Schnapps and some glasses, appeared on a partly demolished bridge which had spanned the River Volturno. He demanded a parley with his British opposite number. That part of the line was held by the 5th Hampshires, and after some delay a company commander walked over to meet the German delegation. For some reason he was accompanied by the battalion padre. The German Hauptmann was courteous, but seemed a bit peeved.

'We have returned five of your stretcher-bearers,' he said. 'Why do you not return ours?'

The British officers explained their point of view, and the orderly filled their glasses. I don't know exactly what turns the conversation took because I wasn't there, but I was told they finished the bottle before resuming hostilities. This fear of fraternization with the enemy showed itself again in an ugly incident on Christmas Day in 1943. We held the little village of Sippiciano and the Germans were just up the road in another village. On Christmas Eve they gave us a splendid firework display of interlacing patterns of tracer in the sky, and on Christmas morning they rang the church bells in their village. The peals sounded clear and sweet on that crisp sunlit day, but the British response was swift and savage. Two aeroplanes appeared high in the sky and as the bombs fell on the German-held village the sound of the bells died away.

On our side the church in Sippiciano was playing an unaccustomed role. We were using it as a field hospital and Geoffrey Parker, our old friend from Salerno, was in charge. Our padre, a Roman Catholic priest called Murphy, was very upset by what he considered to be desecration of a holy place. He had been a missionary in China, but eagerly volunteered for service with the British army when war broke out. He hated the loneliness of his work in China and he loved whisky, playing poker and the fellowship of kindred spirits. However, he was a deeply religious man and could often be seen sitting on an oil drum or an ammunition box, shriving anyone who had a mind to be shriven. He protested violently to our C.O., Lieutenant-Colonel Pitkeathly, about the misuse of the church. The Colonel tried to reason with him.

'Look here, Murphy,' he said, 'it's all very well to talk about consecrated ground. When we took this church over, the floor in front of the altar was covered with shit.'

'Yes it was,' Murphy agreed, and he rose to his feet and pounded the table in his fury, 'but it was British shit.'

In spite of the padre's fine excremental distinctions, the church continued in its secular ministry and Geoff Parker carried out a small operation on me in the body of the kirk. Perhaps this gives me a slight distinction; it's not everybody who's been operated on in a church.

Some time later on in the campaign, I think in July, 1944, Fergus Murphy and I visited Rome together. I couldn't have had a better guide, for Rome was his city and the Chinese Mission his alma mater. We couldn't get a room at the official Transit Hotel so his friends Father Dooley and Father Flynn were kind enough to put us up in the Mission. It was a lovely house and very comfortable, if a trifle overburdened by huge paintings of the Virgin and Child. That evening we went out on the town, and in various bars we fell in with our own C.O., with John O'Connell, an Irish Catholic who was the C.O. of another field ambulance in the division and with our brigade commander, Joe Kendrew, ex rugger captain of England and a triple DSO. After dinner we all went back to the Mission, where we drank and argued into the small hours. The priests were formidable drinkers and great arguers, better than the soldiers on both counts. The next morning we enjoyed the magic of St Peter's and visited St Paul's, where I annoyed Fergus by saying it would make a jolly good dance hall. We separated before midday because John, Fergus and some of the others had an audience with the Pope. As I wasn't part of Il Papa's flock I went off to the Corso Umberto where I bought Thea a pair of silk stockings, and on to the Catacombs. These were largely filled with gum-chewing American G.I.s and as we wound our way through a grim candle-lit vault one of them said to the priest who was showing us round: 'Jeeze! They sure had room for a helluva lotta stiffs in this joint.'

The visit to Rome was a delightful little break in our routine and it came some weeks after the city had been liberated, if that is the right word, by two Allied thrusts, northward from Cassino and eastward from Anzio. We have to go back in time for a few months to return to the subject of water and to another bit of trouble with one of those damned rivers.

Ken Sharp, our Dental Officer and a great friend of mine, was always keen on lending a hand with any bit of excitement that was going, and we had a very nasty problem with a pontoon bridge across the Garigliano. Perhaps Ken thought that 'bridge-work' came within his province. It had been raining for days and the river was in flood. The current was very strong, and masses of flotsam including quite heavy logs were carried down from the upper reaches. As a result some of the pontoons broke loose and the southern end of the bridge, where the current was strongest, was carried away. The ubiquitous Royal Engineers made repeated efforts to rebuild the gap but eventually, after several failures, they ran out of pontoons. Ken and I were on the remains of the bridge, which was still secured to the north bank, and ahead of us the battalions were engaged in quite heavy fighting. About thirty casualties were patiently waiting to be brought across the river to our advanced dressing station half a mile to the rear. Our own stretcher bearers and two of our NCOs were with them. Brigade headquarters was also north of the river and we were effectively cut off. I walked to the HQ and told the Brigadier, who received the news with a visible lack of enthusiasm. Back at the bridge the sappers were still trying; they brought a boat up to the south bank and tied strong ropes to the bow and stern. After several attempts they managed to throw an end of one rope to their mates on our bit of the bridge. The boat was launched from the south bank, controlled by the ropes at either end, and we pulled it across. True to their tradition, the Engineers refused to risk any wounded in the improvised ferry until it had been tested by their own men. The usual two 'volunteers' were detailed to climb down into the boat and the rope party on the south bank hauled away. With the weight of the soldiers the boat settled lower in the water and took the full force of the flood on its beam. It had travelled only a few yards when it capsized and the unfortunate sappers were flung out of the boat and swept away. The upturned boat was hauled back to the remains of the bridge, righted and bailed out, but we were now getting pretty desperate. Somehow, the wounded had to be got across. Ken came up with what seemed to be a possible solution – and one which would certainly have been recommended by any seaman. In later years I often reflected that the Army's antics on water would have been much less lethal if there had been a few seamen around to give advice.

'Why don't you attach both ropes to the bow?' Ken said. 'Let the boat drift downstream from the bridge and then haul it back, bow on to the current, to the south bank.'

The Engineers considered this blinding glimpse of the obvious and came to a swift decision.

'That's a good idea,' they said. 'You thought of it: you try it.'

The sappers re-positioned the ropes and Ken and I, not without some misgivings, got into the boat. Both rope parties eased off the ropes and we whizzed away downstream. Ken's plan worked like a charm and we were hauled back to the bridge.

Two by two, we lowered the wounded into the boat and sent them off on their journey. If Ken and I had been apprehensive, it must have been terrifying for the seriously wounded, especially as by now it was dark and they had no idea where they were going, hearing only the wind and the rushing of the water past the sides of the craft. I remember one man with a shattered and roughly splinted leg being lowered on his stretcher into the boat. The rope parties eased off a bit too quickly and his yell of 'Jesus Christ!' rose above the howling of the wind as he accelerated away into the maelstrom.

It must seem odd to any present-day reader that so many men knew so little about seamanship, but in those days our coasts and lakes were not crowded, as they are now, with amateur sailors and windsurfers. There were no marinas or sea schools, and professional sailors or those with a yen for the sea would have opted to serve in the Royal Navy or mercantile marine. Soldiers, almost by definition, were landlubbers and great credit is due to Ken for solving our little problem from first principles. I can't remember meeting anyone during the war who was interested in sailing, and my own maritime experience was limited to an afternoon with Thea in a rowboat on the Serpentine. Even that was pretty dispiriting because my oarsmanship gave some offence to a huge man who was in another boat with a fat woman. He made some loud and disparaging remarks about my probable ancestry and this in turn so offended Thea that she replied in kind. She was apt to do that. Rather to my alarm he followed us back to the landing stage and it was a great relief to find, when we all disembarked, that he had only one leg.

This ignorance of nautical lore seemed to be equally prevalent in the High Command. Senior officers have always been a bit of a problem, and the higher up you go the worse they get. Brigadiers were reasonably switched on and often retained some vestiges of humanity and common senses but generals, in my experience, were a pretty dodgy lot, and if history is anything to go by, they always have been. Someone should have told our collection that a fully equipped British soldier does not float in water and that an overloaded flat-bottomed canvas boat in a fast-flowing river is very bad news indeed.

I have left until last a little 'bridge' story which perfectly illustrates the instincts of a nation which has often lost battles but hardly ever lost a war. Until recently I thought that perhaps we had lost this spirit, but events in the Falklands have proved me wrong.

When we landed in North Africa the Division was sent to a concentration area where it was reliably predicted that we would all go down with the local version of Gyppy tummy and get that little problem out of our systems. The prediction was correct, and for days we had the most appalling diarrhoea. It was the rainy season, the encampment was inches deep in mud and the flies in the deep trench latrines had never had it so good; there seemed to be millions of them. After about two weeks our temperatures and our bowels returned to normal, and 1st Army HQ pronounced us fit to fight the Germans. I am sorry to report that in this opinion they were not entirely correct. However, in due course we moved up to the front line, around the little mining village of Sedjenane in Tunisia, and our Field Hospital was set up in a railway tunnel. Our stay there was enlivened by the periodic visits of a French army medical officer. He seemed to be running a one-man medical service for which his only equipment was a mule and a rather dirty blanket. He would disappear for days and then materialize with a wounded man wrapped in his blanket and draped over his mule. He would hand over the casualty, accept a meal and demand the return of his blanket; one of ours wouldn't do. Then he would touch his képi in a salute and vanish into the night. I don't know whether he was a regular officer, or who paid him, or what happened to him, but he saved a good many lives.

Just when we were settling down into a fairly regular routine, the Germans saw fit to launch a violent offensive, and I regret to say that we fled precipitately. The Field Hospital was re-established a few miles further back, but our sojourn there was short-lived. At the time I was fortunate in having a truly delightful man, Tommy Farr, as my batman. He modelled himself on P.G. Wodehouse's Jeeves, and everything I possessed was not mine, but 'ours'. It was our socks, our wife, and our everything. He preserved at all times the imperturbable good manners of his hero. One morning he presented himself at my billet and I was surprised to see that he was wearing a steel helmet. He handed me an enamelled mug.

'Your tea, sir,' he said, 'and German tanks are coming down the road.'

Bertie Wooster would have been proud of him, but I jumped about a foot in the air and rushed out into the road. Luckily for us, Tommy was a better batman than military expert. The 'German tanks' were Bren-gun carriers of the Sherwood Foresters and when Tommy saw them they must have been some distance away. However, they were certainly retreating and it seemed that the whole action was degenerating into a rout. I was ordered to pack up and re-establish the Field Hospital a long way — thirty miles — to the rear. I set off on my motorcycle to find a suitable site along roads encumbered by fleeing troops. There was an infectious sense of panic in the air, the kind of panic which can affect raw troops exposed for the first time to the impact of battle. I never saw it again.

When the new Field Hospital was established, I was curious to find out what was happening at the front, and in particular what had happened to our railway tunnel. I rode back on my motorcycle and, as I got nearer to the sounds of war, two tanks lumbered round a bend in the road about a hundred yards ahead. I was not much better at tank-spotting than Tommy and I thought that this time they might really be enemy tanks, so I rode my Matchless into the ditch at the side of the road, jumped off and cowered there while the tanks screeched towards me. I peered cautiously out of the ditch, decided they were on our side and rather shamefacedly dragged the bike out and went on my way.

When I got to the tunnel it was dark, and a spectacular firefight was in progress. The Lincolns had stopped the rot, and all around the entrance to the tunnel they were dug in and blazing away at the enemy. The Krauts were mortaring the whole area and I left my motorcycle at the side of the road and sprinted for the safety of the tunnel. Once it had housed the Field Hospital for the whole brigade, but now it was the Lincolns' regimental aid post. Inside were a lot of wounded being tended by the Battalion Medical Officer, Captain Farquhar. The padre was there and, for some reason which I cannot remember, our own regimental sergeant-major, R.S.M. Baynes. Perhaps, like me, he was just curious. One Austin ambulance was sheltering at the entrance to the tunnel and we crammed it with wounded. The R.S.M. took the wheel and we got the hell out of it. The ambulance was bumping and lurching all over the rough track until we got to the road, and then I followed on my Matchless. It was the last ambulance to leave Sedjenane, for a few hours later the Germans overwhelmed the position.

After the war I met Farquhar when we were both in Edinburgh studying for our Surgical Fellowship, and he told me that the Germans had fired into the tunnel, killing and wounding some of its occupants. He had been shot in the buttock and a ricocheting bullet had carried away the Parson's nose! Everyone in the tunnel was, of course, taken prisoner and some of the wounded, including Farquhar, had to endure a long forced march to a prison camp.

We left the ambulance at the Advanced Dressing Station a mile or so down the road and I nipped back to see how my Field Hospital was getting on. All was well, and the next day my insatiable curiosity took me back to the front. We were still withdrawing, and an Engineer officer stopped me at a bridge.

'You can't go any further,' he said.

'You are going to blow the bridge?' I asked hopefully. At this stage of the war I was eager to learn, and I had never seen a bridge blown.

'No,' he replied. 'I am not. We shall need it when we come back.'

This, on the face of it, very stupid remark typified the inability of the British to admit the possibility of ultimate defeat. He did not blow the bridge, the Germans duly advanced over it and were duly driven back by men of the 16th Parachute Brigade. As the Germans withdrew they demolished the bridge, because, unlike the British, they knew they would not be coming that way again. The Engineer officer was wrong almost to the point of idiocy, but in a curious way he spoke for the whole nation.

I went back to the Field Hospital for the last time, and although it was in a completely safe area the tented operating theatre complex was destroyed a few days later by a bizarre and frightening accident. The surgeon, Major Gledhill, an Australian, was operating on an abdominal wound in the main part of the tent and instruments were being sterilized over a petrol stove in the annexe. The anaesthetic in vogue at the time was ether, a highly inflammable gas, administered by a machine called an Oxford Vaporiser, and the weather was very hot. I happened to be looking in the direction of the operating tent when there was a dull explosion and the whole tent was enveloped in a sheet of flame. Gledhill, his anaesthetist and the rest of the staff staggered out of the inferno, dragging their patient with them, but the man was dead. The flame from the exploding ether had scorched into his lungs. Ammunition pouches taken off earlier patients had been stacked in a corner of the main tent and now began to explode in a violent staccato; soon there was nothing left but a charred mess in the middle of the field.

The anaesthetist bemoaned a peculiar and personal loss. He was Jewish, very dark, and needed to shave twice a day. He had anticipated a possible wartime shortage of razor blades by amassing a vast hoard, which he kept with his other belongings in the theatre complex. Alas, all the blades were annealed in the flames. In the Army it is forbidden, with one or two very rare exceptions, to grow a beard.

Operation Avalanche

Was none who would be foremost
  To lead such dire attack:
But those behind cried 'Forward!'
  And those before cried 'Back!'

Lord Macaulay, commemorating an obstacle on the road to Rome.

Winston Churchill, speaking in the Mansion House on 10 November, 1942, after the battle of El Alamein had been fought and won, made a prophetic comment: 'This is not the end. It is not even the beginning of the end, but it is perhaps the end of the beginning.'

For me there was a specific moment when I knew beyond any doubt that ultimate victory would be ours. It was on 12 May, 1943, and a quarter of a million of the enemy had surrendered unconditionally in Tunisia. I was standing on a road not far from Tunis and watching the scene around me. In a field to my left, hundreds of German soldiers were queueing up for food at one of their mobile field kitchens. Most of them had discarded their shirts and they were in excellent spirits, laughing and joking. In front of me a British corporal was cadging a lift from a German general in an open staff car, and in the distance neat files of steel-helmeted British infantry were marching into the hills to round up enemy stragglers.

The myth of German invincibility had been finally destroyed. Many battles, some bloodier than those already fought, were still to come: Salerno, Anzio, Cassino, Normandy, Arnhem. I knew nothing of that, but I knew that it was now only a matter of time. The mantle of invincibility had passed to us, and we waited impatiently for the time when we would return to the mainland of Europe.

As we waited, and as the months passed with little to do under the blistering North African sun, we entertained ourselves as best we could. I painted a portrait of Thea in watercolour. I copied her face from the photograph I carried in my wallet, and my friend Stanley Hickling modelled her shoulders. Stanley was an extremely muscular young man and some artistic licence was needed in the interpretation. The folds of the dress over her bosom were simulated by a couple of Tunisian oranges slung in a khaki handkerchief from the back of a folding camp chair. Some years later Thea was kind enough to frame the picture, and I have it in my study.

Stanley and I visited Tunis, of which I can remember very little; but I do remember vividly a bizarre scene on a nearby beach. We wanted to swim, but as neither of us had any bathing trunks we retired to the shelter of some rocks and swam lazily and blissfully in the nude. When we had dressed and smoked a cigarette or two we clambered back over the rocks, and there in the middle of the beach was a beefy young Caucasian making very active love to his girlfriend. The amorous pair were completely naked, and this was the odd thing: they were surrounded by a circle of admiring and incredulous Arabs who were squatting in the sand, laughing, smoking their pipes and gesticulating. I doubt if they had ever seen an open-air performance of this particular activity before, and nor for that matter had we. As we walked past, the young man — large in every anatomical sense — brought the affair to an obviously satisfactory conclusion and ran off into the sea to cool down. We glanced at the two piles of discarded clothing and recognized the uniforms and insignia of an American lieutenant and an American army nurse.

Stanley was one of my closest friends and a truly remarkable man. He was not very tall but extremely good-looking, with a quiet voice and a perpetual twinkle in his eye, and he was consumed with boundless energy. Later on, when we were in Italy, he was the only one of us to become fluent in Italian, and this accomplishment stood him in good stead when he was inadvisedly swanning ahead of the advancing army in his jeep and 'liberated' a small Italian town all on his own. Unflappable as usual, and quite unperturbed by his premature arrival, he delivered an eloquent speech from the balcony of the town hall and was warmly applauded by the assembled townsfolk. On his way back he dropped in to an abandoned castle belonging to the Duke of Aosta, and 'borrowed' a couple of elegant chairs for our officers' mess.

When we explored Naples together we were frequently accosted by urchins who offered us a choice from two delicacies they had on offer for the sum of fifty lire: steak and chips, or their sister. Fifty lire was the equivalent of half a crown, or twelve and a half new pence. After declining these offers a number of times we decided that perhaps it might be a good idea to have a look at one of these 'sisters'. Stanley spoke to the next urchin who came up, and we followed the little horror through the back streets of Naples until we came to a house clearly marked 'Out of Bounds to British Troops'. We went in, and up some shabby stairs to a landing where the urchin indicated a couple of wooden chairs. We sat down to wait and I remember feeling rather foolish and vaguely apprehensive. The place was lit by candles because, thanks to the Allied bombing, Naples was without electric light. A very drunk American G.I. came unsteadily and noisily up the stairs, one hand clutching at the rickety banister and the other arm round a scantily clad and rather dispirited looking brunette. Neither of them seemed to notice us and they disappeared down a corridor.

We were beginning to realize that this wasn't turning out quite as we had hoped. Neither of us had been in a brothel before and our sex-starved expectations were along the lines of the plush, velvet-curtained bordellos which were portrayed in American films. The place we were in had all the romantic charisma of a railway waiting room on a disused branch line. Before we could put our misgivings into words a tallish blonde emerged from an adjoining room and swayed gracefully in our direction. She was exquisitely pretty and I hardly noticed the soiled nightdress she was wearing. We hadn't seen a young woman for months, let alone a vision like this. I stared at her lovely eyes, her lips curving sweetly in a shy smile, and her lithe, desirable body. She looked quizzically from one of us to the other, and instinctively we stood up. Her words of welcome were few and to the point, and her voice was shrill and harsh: 'You want-a fuck?'

It is difficult in this permissive age to explain and understand the shocked horror which this matter-of-fact query induced in Stanley and me. Nowadays that particular four-letter word is heard on the radio and television and is used in almost every contemporary novel, along with explicit descriptions of most variants of the act itself. We used plenty of four-letter words ourselves and we were neither prudes nor innocent youths. We were just ordinary young men of our time, and in our world beautiful young women simply did not ask if you wanted a fuck, especially if it was pretty obvious that was exactly what you had in mind. We should have appreciated that the poor girl was unfamiliar with the nuances of the English language, but we didn't. We just snatched up our berets and fled down the stairs pursued by a screech of contemptuous Neapolitan abuse from the angelic-looking creature on the landing.

Some months after this, Stanley came back to Naples to collect the unit's pay from the Field Cashier. It was in occupation currency but it was a sizeable amount of money, and while he was having a drink in a bar the bag was snatched. If I had been in his place I would have been too afraid of a knife in the back to have taken the matter any further, but Stanley pursued the thieves relentlessly through the slums of Naples, losing their trail from time to time but picking it up again by threats and by his command of the language. He was alone and unarmed, but he eventually tracked the miscreants down and then, with the aid of the military police, recovered the money.

However, all this was yet to come. For the time being we were stuck in North Africa and getting extremely bored. A notice appeared in Daily Routine Orders inviting applications to join a new unit called the Special Air Service.* We had never heard of it, but although I cannot recall the exact wording of the notice it seemed to promise some relief from our boredom. Stanley and I applied, and a few weeks later we were accepted. It was not clear from the signal whether we would be employed as doctors or combatants but it was absolutely clear that we would have to relinquish our respective ranks and revert to lieutenant. Stanley was a captain and I was a major, and while we were not over-bothered about the rank,

---

* Twenty-six years later our only son, more determined than I, gave up his studies as a medical student and really did join the S.A.S.

the loss of pay would be an unexpected blow to our wives at home. We were still pondering this unsatisfactory state of affairs when we were given an opportunity to decline, without loss of face, the kind offer from the S.A.S. We were let off the hook by the news that our Division, the 46th, was to spearhead an invasion of Europe.

There followed a period of intense activity as we were trained in the techniques of amphibious warfare. We embarked in landing craft, disembarked and dashed up beaches; we watched an impressive demonstration of a rocket ship in action; we became extremely fit and we attended numerous conferences. At one of these we were addressed by an American admiral who seemed to be in charge of our travel arrangements. He said he would guarantee to land us in the right country but he could not be sure that we would be in the right place. It was nice to find an admiral with a sense of humour and we all laughed. None of us was sufficiently experienced in the art of beach-finding to realize that he was not joking.

At this time I was second-in-command of 185 Field Ambulance, attached to 128 (Hampshire) Infantry Brigade, which was part of the 46th Division. The shoulder emblem of the 46th was an oak tree, 'which may sway, but never breaks'. Nor did it.

The main duty of a field ambulance was to collect casualties from the regimental aid posts (RAPs) of the three battalions in the brigade and remove them as rapidly as possible from the battlefield, augmenting if necessary the first-aid and anti-shock treatment already given in the RAPs.

The field ambulance had three components: a headquarters, which established the main dressing station (MDS) and two companies, A Coy and B Coy, either of which could establish an advanced dressing station (ADS) and provide stretcher-bearers for collecting casualties from the RAPs. The companies would leapfrog each other to conform with the advance or withdrawal of the fighting troops. There were no surgeons on the establishment of a field ambulance, but if one or more field surgical units (FSUs) were attached to the MDS, it then became a Field Hospital.

Casualties were moved from the ADS to the MDS by motor ambulance, but movement between the RAPs and the ADS varied according to the distances involved and the nature of the terrain.

The distance on a beach in the initial stages of a landing would be very short, a matter of yards, while in the mountains it could be six or seven miles.

Sometimes it was possible to use a motor ambulance, but more often the seriously wounded were carried by hand on stretchers, a method which was comfortable for the wounded but painfully slow, or by jeeps adapted to carry stretchers. The jeep was fast but gave the wounded man a very rough and uncomfortable ride, especially if, because of enemy action, the driver was anxious to leave the district at soon as possible. We also tried mules, with two casualties slung in panniers on either side of the animal or one perched on top. The mules belied their reputation for obstinacy and proved to be docile and willing beasts, but for the patients they were neither particularly fast nor, as they picked their way along steep narrow tracks in the mountains, did they inspire any great confidence. All too often there were rocky outcrops on one side and a nasty drop on the other.

The personnel of a field ambulance consisted of over two hundred RAMC all ranks, and about eighty RASC, who were responsible for the motor transport and for armed defence of the unit. There were nine doctors including the commanding officer and the two company commanders, one dentist, one chaplain, one transport officer and a quartermaster. The duties of the commanding officer, and the main duties of the company commanders, were administrative and tactical rather than clinical. It was necessary for all three to be in close contact with the combatants and to understand the conduct and progress of any fighting. Their job was to ensure that casualties were evacuated as speedily as possible to and from dressing stations which had to be correctly sited, accommodated and moved to new locations as the need arose. If the MDS had no FSU attached and was not acting as a Field Hospital the wounded were evacuated to a casualty clearing station (CCS).

In battle the main objective of a field ambulance can be summed up in a few words: it is to bring the wounded to a surgeon in the shortest possible time and in the best possible condition. This, too, should be the objective of the overall medical plan.

The conferences went on and numerous decisions were taken which involved us to more or less degree. The operation was code-named AVALANCHE and the Division's assaulting brigade was to be our own — 128 Infantry Brigade. We would therefore be landing with the assault troops and would be responsible for establishing the initial medical arrangements in the Divisional beachhead. The whole unit would not be required at first, but a total of 202 all ranks, mixed RAMC and RASC, were allotted places in craft which would off-load at intervals during the first few hours. The unit was of necessity fragmented and would embark in eighteen craft of various types. Because of this fragmentation it was decided that I would land with the first wave of assaulting infantry, with the commendable intention of assembling and co-ordinating each detachment as it landed. In the event things did not work out exactly according to plan. They never do. Officers down to the rank of major were shown aerial photographs of the target beach, and we saw a network of lanes giving access inland. Because of these lanes and bearing in mind my duties as co-ordinator, I made two decisions all on my own. I decided to take a bicycle and to strap on to its carrier a hoarded bottle of whisky. I felt sure that this would be of some medicinal value.

Once ashore our orders were crystal clear — in theory. A section of our men would land with each of the assaulting battalions and would help the regimental stretcher-bearers to collect the wounded into what were rather insensitively called 'dumps' on the beach. When the ADS was established, the dumps of wounded would be moved there and would be retained until they could be evacuated to the MDS as soon as that, in turn, was open for business. Two field surgical units, each consisting of a surgeon, anaesthetist and supporting staff, would be attached in due course to the MDS, which would then function as a field hospital and be responsible for all surgery within the Divisional perimeter until such time as a CCS was ashore and operational.

Evacuation from the Field Hospital would be to the medical section of a Divisional beach organization called, for some obscure reason, a 'Beach Brick'. The Beach Brick would arrange evacuation by sea to hospital ships and similar craft called hospital carriers lying offshore. These were all converted merchantmen.

At the time these orders seemed to be pretty sensible and it never occurred to us to question them, or to seek their amendment or elaboration. A pleasant young man from the staff of Combined Operations Headquarters was attached to us to give us the benefit of his advice, but as he had never heard a shot fired in anger nobody took any notice of the poor chap.

On 5 September, 1943, we embarked in the armada of vessels anchored off the Tunisian port of Bizerta and sailed to Sicily, harbouring briefly off the north-west coast of the island. Here all ranks were briefed and our exact destination made known. We were to land on beaches in the Gulf of Salerno, just south of Naples.

In the meantime two events had occurred which altered my personal role and status in the impending fracas. The senior medical officer of the Division was recalled unexpectedly to England and my C.O., Lieutenant-Colonel A. J. Pitkeathly, was appointed in his place. Automatically therefore, command of our own unit devolved upon me. At the time I was rather pleased, and I assume that I must have exercised some control over affairs during the next few weeks, but I cannot recall making a single decision which materially influenced the course of events. I remember only that as the battle wore on I became increasingly aware of personal failure, failure which had nothing to do with the performance of those under my command, who carried out their duties with courage, resolution and skill. Wisdom after the event is not an attractive attribute, but at the end of this chapter I will try to analyse what went wrong. First, however, I will set down my recollections of the actual landing and of incidents which, though trivial and unimportant in themselves, may convey some sense of the confusion which prevailed upon that awful beach.

We clambered down the nets which had been slung over the side of the US Navy transport and dropped into the ugly flat-bottomed barges waiting below. Each barge held about forty men and I was with a platoon of the 5th Battalion the Hampshire Regiment; I think it was No. 9 Platoon. My bicycle was lowered down, and both it and the whisky bottle tied to its carrier came in for some ribald comment. I peered over the side into the darkness: there were other similar craft on either side, LCAs (landing craft assault).

For an hour we idled to and fro on the gentle swell while the rest of the transports discharged their human cargo. The quiet throb of the engine mingled with the clink of weapons and an occasional curse or uneasy quip from my companions. At some signal we began to move, slowly at first until we were in line abreast, then faster, towards the unseen shore five or so miles away. I found a foothold on the side of the hull and levered myself up to have a look. The bow waves of the speeding craft showed up clearly in the moonlight, a few on our right and many more on our left. The first wave of LCAs was a minute ahead of us, and behind us would come the big LCIs, crowded with infantry; behind them the LCTs and LSTs loaded down with transport and artillery. Operation AVALANCHE was under way.

I remember this as a long-awaited and deeply emotional moment. The tide of war had turned and we were on our way to drive the enemy from the mainland of Europe. A few hours earlier the news of Italy's capitulation had been broadcast to the fleet and we thought that our landing would be unopposed. Morale was high, but bitter disillusion was just fifteen minutes away.

On the passage from Bizerta I had shared a cabin with Bob, the platoon commander, a tough professional soldier. He had been a sergeant in the Scots Guards and was recently commissioned. This was his first command in battle and he was at the front of the LCA with another Hampshire officer. I was right at the back and just behind me an American naval lieutenant, an ex-Harvard man, was at the helm, sitting on the small raised afterdeck. We were coming in on a compass bearing but his eyes strained ahead, looking for the lights which were to guide us in. Suddenly he called out that he had seen a light to starboard. We were nearly there. At about the same moment lines of tracer reached out lazily towards us and bullets smacked harmlessly against the hull. Another minute or so and we came to a grinding halt as we hit the beach and the ramp crashed down. The tracer was still coming, and a soldier beside Bob was hit. His body toppled into the water, and with shocked surprise we heard voices shouting in German. There was a fleeting moment, it seemed an eternity, when everyone froze. The soldiers in front stared at the half-submerged body of their comrade and suddenly the American behind me, his nerves strained to breaking point, screamed 'For Christ's sake get off!'

That instant of time remains with me still, and always reminds me of Macaulay's tale of how Horatius kept the bridge as the ranks of Tuscany pressed down upon him. They didn't like what they saw either: 'But those behind cried Forward!, and those before cried Back!'

Bob broke the spell, and the moment passed.

'Come on,' he yelled, and we crowded down the ramp into the water. It was not very deep, and I hauled my bicycle after me. The darkness and the ghostly beauty of an hour before had given place to a fury of light and sound. The Germans were ready for us and had trained every gun and mortar on to the beach. The machine gunners had altered their traverse and a deadly criss-cross of tracer lay just ahead. A Royal Navy rocket ship sent in a clutch of missiles and the flickering fire of a burning building lit up the skyline. I could see the crouching figures of Bob and his men groping their way forward, silhouetted against the kaleidoscope of high explosive. They disappeared into the distance and I never saw Bob again.

When we were leaving the LCA the soldier in front of me caught some part of his equipment in the front wheel of my bicycle. He made a succinct comment on my intelligence and ancestry but I didn't think it was the time or place to reason with him. However, now that we were ashore I began to see his point of view. The heavy army bicycle was indeed an infernal nuisance and was making me a bit conspicuous. I was unique – the only chap on Salerno beach with a bicycle – so I waded back into the sea and threw the machine into deep water. Then I remembered the whisky.

Back on dry land I crouched down behind a heap of debris and wondered what to do next. There did not seem to be any immediate demand for my services as a co-ordinator. Two figures materialized a few yards away, bent nearly double like everyone else, but making their way *towards* the sea. They were German soldiers, captured and disarmed by Bob and his men. When they reached the water's edge they stopped and conferred with each other. They were in the same predicament as I was, wondering what they ought to be doing. They hadn't seen me and after a few moments they turned and began to go back towards their own lines. I stood up and took my revolver from its holster. I had never fired it in anger, and now reflected that I wasn't paid to shoot German soldiers in the back. It would have been easy to take them prisoner again but what on earth was I to do with them? In the prevailing atmosphere of seaside mayhem I was more concerned with staying alive than standing guard over a couple of Krauts. I suppose I ought to have done something, but whilst I still hesitated they disappeared into the smoke. I have often wondered what became of them and whether they survived the return journey.

I began to work my way forward, hoping to see some landmark which would give a clue to our exact position. Bob had silenced at least one of the machine-gun posts and more troops were coming ashore. I stumbled and nearly fell, and looking down I saw that my foot had caught in the trip wire of an anti-personnel mine. It must have been faulty.

'Holy shit!' I thought, and moved on again, barely conscious of my reprieve. The first glimmerings of dawn showed a low stone wall twenty yards ahead with a dozen soldiers taking cover beside it. There was no wall like this on the aerial photographs and I couldn't recognize any other feature. It was getting lighter by the minute and some of the soldiers sheltering by the wall produced packets of cigarettes.

Almost to my surprise, our own men and equipment began to arrive. Captain Dai David, a tough thickset Welshman who got an M.C. later on in the campaign, was crawling over the sand towards us.

'There's an armistice with the Eye-ties,' he shouted cheerfully. Dai always looked on the bright side.

Where the low stone wall ended on the left there was a footpath leading inland and flanking a much higher wall which looked as though it might surround a big garden. An officer and a number of men were sheltering in front of it, and the officer pointed to a building at the end of the footpath.

'Watch out!' he shouted. 'There's a sniper in there.'

'Why don't you shoot the bugger?' I yelled back.

The high wall gave quite good cover, and we set up a rudimentary dressing station. Someone told me there was a bullet hole in my pack, and I took it off to have a look. A bullet had passed right through the pack from side to side, mangling my mess tin on the way.

It was now apparent to everyone who had seen the aerial photographs that the American admiral in Tunis had not been joking. We were indeed in the right country but in the wrong place. The big landing craft were coming in and men began pushing huge rolls of wire netting over the sand so that vehicles would not bog down. Some jeeps were coming ashore, but there was no way off the beach. The anticipated network of lanes was somewhere else, and now that it was light any kind of gap was accurately registered by the German gunners and snipers. No. 9 Platoon, and many of the troops who had carried out the initial assault in the dark, were somewhere inland but no one seemed to know what had happened to them. Heavy shelling of the beach continued without respite, some of the landing craft had been hit and morale was very low. I think that if the enemy had been able to put in a determined infantry attack on the beach we would have surrendered.

I wandered off to try and find out what was going on. I saw a stationary jeep with a figure hanging out of the driver's seat. I recognized the man as an officer I knew in the RAOC. He was terribly wounded and I lifted him, or what was left of him, back into the seat. His face was ashen, but he smiled his thanks. I don't think he knew that he was dying. I kept moving to the left, northwards along the beach. Most of the activity seemed to be in that direction but nobody could tell me anything definite. I came up behind two soldiers lying on a little ridge. They seemed to be looking over the edge, but I couldn't see their faces because of the packs on their backs.

'Have you seen Brigade HQ?' I asked.

There was no reply and I prodded one of them with my foot. He didn't move and I took a closer look. The 'ridge' was the edge of a shell crater and the men were headless. I turned away in horror and looked out to sea. A small landing craft was pulling away from the shore, its task accomplished. As I watched it was suddenly enveloped in a great plume of spray, and in a moment it was gone. There was nothing, not even any debris, nothing. Further along the beach an LST was on fire with flames and dense smoke erupting from amidships, but vehicles were still being driven down its ramp and there was a flurry of men dragging equipment from the stricken vessel.

Eventually I found Brigade HQ – about as rudimentary as our dressing station and just as confused. We were to move, everybody was to move, northward along the beach to where we should have been in the first place. I got back to the dressing station as quickly as I could. More of our personnel and equipment had arrived but there were many wounded, all of them in need of the surgery we were unable to provide. The corporal cook was brewing a dixie of tea on a petrol stove and when he heard a shell coming uncomfortably close he flung his body across the container to protect its precious contents. This splendid act of self-sacrifice and devotion to duty earned him the only good laugh of the day.

'Well done, Corp!' somebody shouted.

We began hailing the commanders of any craft which had unloaded and asked them to take off our wounded. They were not terribly keen on hanging about while the stretcher-bearers made their laborious way down the beach and I had a furious argument with one of them, but in the end sixty-one casualties got away and we started the northward trek along the beach, carrying what equipment we had and taking the remaining wounded with us.

After a few hundred yards we met an RAF officer. He was very smart in a neatly creased light blue battledress and a service dress cap. He carried no pack or other equipment and he might have been on his way to the Mess for a drink, except that he had a revolver in his right hand. He waved it languidly at a group of a dozen excitable Italian soldiers who were jumping about in the background.

'Would you mind taking these fellows along with you, old chap?'

I was so taken aback that I agreed without demur. I did not even ask him where he had found the Italians, or what he was doing on the beach without an aeroplane. We put the Italians to work carrying some of the equipment and straggled on again, but a soldier with his foot blown off shouted a warning to us that we were walking into a minefield. One of his mates was crawling towards him, using a bayonet as a mine detector, and two of our stretcher bearers stayed behind to lend a hand. I decided that we would walk along the bed of a little stream which was winding across the beach. No one would have laid any mines in the stream. The Italians were very reluctant to get their feet wet and had to be persuaded, rather roughly, to do as they were told.

At last we reached the new Brigade area and the men began to set up the tented dressing station which for more than a week was to be the only 'hospital' for the sick and wounded of the 46th Division. It was in a vineyard about 700 yards from the beach and we were joined in due course by the two field surgical units. During the next ten days 1,839 casualties were admitted to this little hospital – 351 sick and 1,488 wounded. This did not include the sixty-one wounded evacuated directly from the beach, nor do the figures give any indication of the number killed in action. Many of the wounded were lying on stretchers in the open, plagued by flies in the daytime and by mosquitoes and other insects at night.

Forty-four men died in the hospital and 192 of the most seriously wounded were operated on by the two surgeons, Major A.K. Price and Major Geoffrey Parker of 23 and 24 FSUs respectively. All survivors were eventually evacuated by sea to Bizerta, Philippeville and Tripoli.

Within the perimeter order and morale were slowly restored. Troops and equipment poured into the beachhead, and the Division nibbled away at the ring of enemy positions. The success of the landing, for it was a success in the end, owed less to the planners than to the stubborn fighting qualities of the men from Hampshire, to Bob and his kind who had advanced without flinching through a murderous curtain of fire to grapple with a hidden enemy and hold him down long enough to let their comrades pull themselves together and gather strength, and their wits, for the morrow.

As the brigade fought its way into the surrounding hills there was a new sense of confusion. The narrow roads were so tortuous that peace gave place to war, and war to peace, in bewildering sequence. In some tumbledown house a black-clad peasant woman would be pounding away at the weekly wash whilst round the next bend would come the sudden staccato of a fire-fight, the short sharp burst of a German Spandau mingling with the slower rhythm of the Brens. Sometimes, to make confusion worse, the Germans would use a captured Bren.

This absence of a stabilized 'front line' was nearly my undoing. About seven days after the landing I was riding a motorcycle along one of these winding roads on my way to a little village called Mercatello where we were going to establish an ADS. I came round a corner and saw a dozen or so German soldiers a hundred yards away. Prisoners, I thought.

I was moving at about thirty mph and two other thoughts came to me in rapid succession: first, that the Germans were carrying a wounded comrade on some kind of stretcher and, second, that they were armed and wearing steel helmets. I knew from past experience that one of the first things a Kraut did when he was taken prisoner was to throw away his helmet and put on his peaked forage cap. By the time my mind had digested these impressions I was about twenty yards away and it was too late to turn back. I opened the throttle wide and roared through them.

I didn't see the expression on any of their faces. The next bend was a hundred yards further on and I crouched low over the handlebars. I could feel the hair rising on the back of my neck as I waited for the shots. Nothing happened, and I tore round the next two bends. There was an olive grove on the left. I slithered into it, leapt off the machine and began frantically to wipe away the chinagraph markings on my map cover. They showed the positions of every unit in the brigade and by this time I was beginning to think that I had strayed into enemy territory. However, once I had got the telltale markings off the map I checked again and was sure I was on the right road.

A group of Italians came out of the nearby farmhouse. They were very excited and beckoned me to follow them. They took me over to a haystack and one of them burrowed into its centre. He came out holding a Schmeisser sub-machine gun which he proudly presented to me. He pointed up the road in the direction the Germans had taken and I heard the word '*Tedeschi*'. Obviously they wanted me to go back and fight, and although I tried to explain that I was a man of peace I'm afraid they were sadly disappointed in me. I left my motorcycle at the farm and continued on foot. Half a mile further on I came across two Hampshire soldiers lying dead in the road. The canvas hood of their 15 cwt truck was still smouldering. Like me, they had been surprised by the German fighting patrol. Perhaps they had been ambushed, but with odds of six to one against them they had fought to the death and wounded one of the enemy, the man on the stretcher.

I went to Brigade HQ to report what I had seen. The Brigade Commander grunted non-committally and asked his gunners if they could put some fire down on the estimated position of the patrol, on the Germans who for some unaccountable reason had spared my life. That evening my friend Ken Sharp, the Dental Officer, came with me to retrieve the motorcycle.

Most of the Italian soldiers whom we had inherited from the RAF officer slipped away during the next few days and we made no effort to detain them, but two of them stayed with us for many months. They wanted to rejoin their families in a village far to the north, and they worked hard and cheerfully for their British army rations. I heard them use only two English phrases ... 'Choppy up' and 'Fuck off!' but their limited grasp of our language and way of life seemed to meet all their needs. I think they were very popular, and when we got within reach of their village they shook hands all round, packed up their few belongings, and left.

The next morning one of them was back, and we found him at first light. He was hanging by a rope around his neck from a tree in the bivouac area. We never knew what tragedy the poor boy had found on reaching home, or why he chose to die with us. We buried him as we would have buried one of our own.

Wisdom After The Event

The main objective of a field ambulance is to bring the wounded to a surgeon in the shortest possible time and in the best possible condition. At Salerno the medical services failed to achieve this objective and the memory of those soldiers lying in the vineyard has been on my conscience for over forty years. I do not know whether the planners took note of the failure and profited by it, but for us in the field there was no time for the luxury of self-analysis. Each day brought fresh tasks and new problems to overcome as best we could. Now I can ponder the events of long ago and consult the War Diaries which I and many others wrote on the beaches and in the ships, and I can read again the orders which were issued by Divisional and Army Headquarters. They are all preserved and filed away in the Public Record Office and can be regurgitated at the touch of a button. Where did we go wrong and who was to blame?

We embarked at Bizerta with 202 officers and men and our casualties during the landing, two killed and eight wounded, could have been much worse. Even so, the strength of the unit, already pared down for the landing, was reduced to 192. The number of doctors was reduced by a third because our Colonel was acting as A.D.M.S., another doctor, Captain Eric Steel, was wounded, and the officer who should have been in charge of the M.D.S., Major Douglas MacRae, was seriously indisposed throughout the action. The remaining officers and men worked like demons, and I remember with particular respect the untiring and devoted efforts of Captain Alec Porterfield who was in effective charge of the M.D.S., and of our regimental sergeant-major, R.S.M. Baynes. It was in no way their fault that the M.D.S. was overwhelmed, but I could have done far more than I did to help them. I should have demanded additional help from other field ambulance resources which were soon ashore and available, but which were held in reserve until we were relieved on the tenth day.

The work of the two field surgical units was of course crucial to the whole medical plan, but for a variety of reasons they did not become operational in the vineyard until thirty-six hours after the landing. A surgical team with one surgeon and one anaesthetist can deal, on average, with a dozen major operations every twenty-four hours, and our two surgeons* carried out 192 operations in eight days. If we include the casualties evacuated directly from the beach it is clear that 1,357 men were *not* operated on within the Divisional perimeter. It was madness to expect these two surgeons, of necessity arriving late on the scene, to cope with the backlog of casualties from a brigade which had been bloodily engaged for thirty-six hours with a resolute and formidable enemy. What happened to those 1,357 men, nearly all from our division, who could not be operated on at the Field Hospital? Orders from 46 Div. HQ had envisaged that casualties would be transferred, by unspecified means, to hospital ships and hospital carriers and evacuated to Sicily. In the event they had a much longer voyage either to Bizerta in Tunisia, Philippeville in Algeria or Tripoli in Libya. 5th Army Orders detailed four hospital ships and three hospital carriers to cover the operation and one of these vessels, the hospital carrier *St David*, was to be on station in the Gulf of Salerno on D-Day. She duly arrived on the morning of D-Day, 9 September, reporting to the Naval Control Ship, HMS *Hilary*, at 1020 hrs and at 1400 hrs she moved closer to the shore and began to embark casualties directly from the beach. She sailed from the Gulf at 0600 hrs the following morning, some twenty-six hours after the first troops had landed, with a load of 283 casualties. Many of the men were severely

---

* One of the two surgeons, Geoffrey Parker, worked with us for many months and became our very good friend. He was a first-class surgeon and a man of great courage and resource. In 1944 he parachuted into occupied France to act as surgeon to the Maquis operating in the mountains of the High Jura. For this he was awarded the DSO and Croix de Guerre, and was made a Commander of the Légion d'Honneur. He wrote a fascinating and exciting book entitled *The Black Scalpel*, so called because of the black Commando dagger he carried – and used. In the preamble to his book he described Salerno as the nearest thing to hell on earth that he had ever experienced.

wounded and twenty died during the thirty-six hour passage to Philippeville. The next medical vessel to arrive in the Gulf, fifty-two hours after the assault had begun, was the hospital ship *Somersetshire*. It took twelve hours to embark a full load of 441 casualties and the ship then sailed for Philippeville where she docked forty-eight hours later, five full days after the initial landing. The patients were disembarked and transferred to a shore hospital where they awaited their turn for surgery.

Three more hospital ships and five hospital carriers eventually arrived in the Gulf and did sterling work from then on. Some of them, although conspicuously marked by day and by night, were viciously attacked by the Luftwaffe, and one, the hospital ship *Newfoundland*, was sunk with the loss of twenty-one lives. All these ships were converted merchantmen, manned by merchant seamen and staffed by British army surgeons, British and American army nurses, and RAMC other ranks. Army policy was to use them for transport only, not as floating front-line operating theatres. Regrettably, there was a total lack of preliminary liaison between the land and maritime medical services. When the hospital ship *Aba* arrived on the third day the outspoken senior medical officer on board, Lieutenant-Colonel P. Lloyd-Williams, reported that briefings of the hospital ships were hopelessly inadequate and that the senior medical officer of the beach organization (the Beach Brick) knew nothing about the arrangements for hospital ships.

With hindsight it is easy to see that floating operating theatres should have been provided on hospital ships standing offshore from the very beginning, and that casualties should have been evacuated direct from shore to these ships until such time as hospital facilities with three or four surgical teams per division had been established ashore. The problem of beach-to-ship transfer must have been in the minds of the planners at some stage because at least three of the hospital carriers, the *Leinster*, the *St David*, and the *St Julien*, were equipped with water ambulances. These were flat-bottomed wooden craft which could come close inshore and could be winched up to deck level on the parent ship. They appear to have been used by the *St David* on D-Day. We failed in our prime objective of bringing the wounded to a surgeon in the shortest possible time and the best possible condition because we relied from the outset on quantitatively inadequate land-based surgical facilities. There was no clear appreciation of the difficulties which attend the treatment and evacuation of casualties sustained during the initial phase of an opposed landing on an enemy shore. Above all, nobody seemed to remember the basic principle that a sufficient number of surgeons must be operational and reasonably accessible before the enemy is engaged. This principle was well understood on land but, because the Mediterranean and Tyrrhenian Seas intervened between our base and our objective, it was totally ignored. My own personal failure lay in my preoccupation with the fluid nature of the fighting on the perimeter, to the neglect of the far more important medical situation in the Field Hospital. I should have recognized the impossible conditions under which Alec Porterfield and his men were working, and should have insisted on help from the resources which were available.

It is interesting to contrast the medical arrangements at Salerno with those for the Falklands campaign. When the Paras and the Commandos waded ashore at San Carlos on 21 May, 1982, the anchorage behind them was dominated by SS *Canberra*, the 'Great White Whale'. Operating theatres on board were staffed and ready, and two Royal Naval surgical teams were standing by to deal with the twenty-four casualties which were transferred to the ship that day. Further out to sea the hospital ship *Uganda* was an ocean-going hospital with magnificent equipment and departments fully staffed with consultants in every relevant speciality. There were, in addition, surgical teams in HMS *Hermes*, HMS *Invincible*, and in one of the ships of the Royal Fleet Auxiliary.

The troops who landed to repossess the islands were fortunate in one respect: the initial landings were virtually unopposed, and the six days which elapsed before the attack on Goose Green enabled a main dressing station and field hospital to be established in a disused refrigeration plant at Ajax Bay. Had there been determined opposition in the San Carlos beachhead the medical support teams might have faced some of the difficulties which confronted us at Salerno. *Canberra* could not have remained in the vicinity because she was basically a troopship with hospital facilities, and had no right to protection under the Geneva Convention. In the event she was withdrawn because of the danger from air attack and the need to bring 5 Brigade from South Georgia. However, the contrast between the two operations is inescapable. In the Falklands, by good planning and with a bit of luck, surgical facilities were in being *before* casualties were sustained. At Salerno they were not. In 1943 most of the wounded had to endure a long sea voyage before receiving definitive treatment. Many died in transit and forty-four died in the field hospital. Only two died in Ajax Bay, and only two in *Uganda*.

Our casualties at Salerno were, of course, far more numerous than in the Falklands, but heavy losses were surely anticipated, and I feel that Salerno must go down in history as a medical disaster.

The Crossing of the Rapido

Our bugles sang truce − for the night cloud had lowered
And the sentinel stars set their watch in the sky;
And thousands had sunk on the ground overpowered,
The weary to sleep, and the wounded to die.

Thomas Campbell

The best laid schemes o' mice an' men
Gang aft a-gley

Robert Burns

The First World War started, so they say, because Archduke Ferdinand's chauffeur took the wrong road, and while he was reversing his car to get back on course the assassin had time to take careful and accurate aim. On a rather less momentous occasion I once led a convoy of forty army lorries down a narrow cul-de-sac. Anyone who has made a similar mistake will know that the British squaddy is at his conversational best when his officer has made an idiot of himself. Ever since that day I have been obsessed with the necessity of not losing my way, and this obsession had some relevance to the tiny part I played in one of the great battles of the Second World War.

When the Allied armies streamed northwards after their successful landings in the south of Italy they were halted at Cassino − the gateway to Rome and beyond. For six long months they prowled around this fearful place, sometimes dashing themselves against its seemingly impregnable defences, only to be bloodily repulsed. Battalion after battalion, brigade after brigade, division after division − New Zealand, Indian, British and American − each in turn was decimated by the stubborn, courageous and skilful defenders. The Germans had every possible advantage of terrain and they used it well. The main road from the south − Highway

Six, we called it – pointed like an arrow to the heap of rubble which once had been the town of Cassino. Behind and to the right was the towering mass of Monte Cassino crowned by the ruins of the Benedictine Abbey. To the left was another mass of mountains stretching away to the sea, and in between there was a gap about three miles wide. The gap was spanned by a little river called, with good reason, the Rapido, and beyond we could see the Liri Valley and the road to Rome.

By 11 May, 1944, General Alexander had assembled a mighty force to punch through this little gap: a quarter of a million men, 1,600 guns, 2,000 tanks and 3,000 aircraft. He had done more than that. So cleverly had he concealed his preparations and so bemused the Germans by his decoys, deceptions and cover plans that they thought themselves confronted by less than half these numbers. Some of their divisions had been taken north in anticipation of a suspected Allied seaborne landing, and because of the apparent stalemate at Cassino one of the senior German commanders had gone on leave. Alexander's plan for the attack was simple but comprehensive. The British and Commonwealth divisions were to hurl themselves into the gap, and into the Liri Valley, by crossing the Rapido. The Poles, thirsting for revenge against their hated enemy, were to seize the corpse-strewn heights on the right – and these two thrusts would pinch out Cassino itself. The French colonial troops, with their redoubtable Arab Goumiers, would take the heights on the left of the gap and further west the Americans would fight their way on to the coast road.

The world knows the outcome of this fierce and bloody encounter and its terrible scars have healed. The monastery has been rebuilt, the town of Cassino lives again and a huge cemetery remains for all to see, and sometimes perhaps to remember, the 185,000 who were killed or wounded in this awful place. My story is concerned with just two hundred yards of the River Rapido, and tells of how important it can be not to lose one's way in the dark.

For four days we had been hiding in the hills, thousands of us with nothing to do but keep out of sight and prepare quietly and unobtrusively for what was to come. My unit, 185 Field Ambulance, had been loaned to 28 Infantry Brigade, who were to cross the river that night. Our commanders knew, but we did not, that four months earlier the American 36th Division had been destroyed in an attempt to cross the river at the very same place. The American casualties had been so heavy that they caused a Congressional inquiry.

A soldier was sitting in front of his little bivouac tent beside me. He was polishing his bayonet with feverish intensity, chattering and laughing with his friends. He had fair hair, cut short and bleached by the sun, and a very pleasant cheerful face. I put down the novel Thea had sent me and watched him. He seemed a very likeable boy, honest and kind. He looked up and grinned at me with a sort of bravado. I knew what he was thinking. All that polishing of his bayonet was just a sham: he didn't want to stick it into anybody and he'd been laughing and talking a bit too much. This was probably his first battle and he was wondering how he was going to behave. He was hoping that he would do well, that he would show no fear in front of his comrades and he was hoping that he would stay alive and that if he were to be wounded it wouldn't be too bad. Soon he would try to get a few hours sleep, and he would think of his parents and his girlfriend and of the village or town or street he had left behind.

I took up my book again, but I didn't see the words. I, too, wondered what the morrow would bring. Had I done everything that was required of me? Was anything forgotten? In my mind I went over the plans again. They were simple enough: plans always were, but would we be able to carry them out? It was lucky for me that I had no gift of prescience: like the rest of us I just did, or tried to do, what I was told. The orders were clear: The 2nd Bn the King's (Liverpool) Regiment would cross the river in canvas assault boats, about eight men to a boat, at two crossing places a hundred or so yards apart and would secure the first objective on the enemy side of the river. The 2nd Bn the Somerset Light Infantry would then cross, pass through the King's, and secure the second objective. The third battalion of the brigade, the 2nd/4th Hampshires, would be in reserve and some of them would man the ferries, forty boats in all. I have forgotten what the objectives were. They didn't concern me and in the event neither of them was taken that night.

I was to go down to the river with one company of my unit. I had two officers, half-a-dozen NCOs and fifty-six stretcher-bearers. Casualties, so it was planned, would be brought to the regimental aid posts on the far side of the river and ferried across to the near side where our stretcher-bearers would collect them, carry them a couple of hundred yards to the lane which ran parallel to the river and load them on to jeeps converted to carry stretchers. The jeeps would be driven away, at first parallel to the river, then turning left into the hills where we now sat and where our advanced dressing station was already established.

No movement had been allowed during daylight, but the night before I had carried out a careful reconnaissance down to the river bank, memorizing every detail of the track and every turning. No way was I going to get lost. Military orders are usually given twice, by a verbal briefing and then by a confirmatory written order. However, this plan was so simple that I tossed the written orders aside, unread. There was little to remember and I knew the way. At 2300 hrs there would fall upon the unsuspecting Germans an artillery barrage the like of which had never been seen or heard before. At the centre, in the British and Commonwealth sector, a thousand guns, all targeted on enemy strongpoints, would blaze away for forty minutes. It was assumed that this deluge of high explosive would keep their heads down while the boats were carried to the river and the leading infantry assembled and embarked at the two crossing points. The timing of the approach march was therefore vital. Too soon and the movement might be detected, too late and the barrage would have lifted.

At the calculated time we set off, the long files of the King's in front of my little detachment and the Somersets behind me. At 2300 hrs precisely the awesome thunder of the guns began, the horizon behind us flickered continuously and the shells whined and whistled overhead. After some distance − I can't remember how far − we came to a fork in the track and I saw to my dismay that the battalion ahead of me had swung to the left. I sprinted ahead until I found an officer.

'You're going the wrong way,' I told him.

'No we're not; the route is in the orders.'

We argued for a few moments while his men marched past us, but he'd had his orders and that was that.

'I don't give a sod what you think,' I said. 'I'm turning right.'

We left the battalions and went on down the tracks I had memorized so carefully and we got to the river on time.

Some Royal Engineers and the detachment from the Hampshires had carried the boats, standard folding assault craft made of canvas and wood, down to the river from the assembly point near the lane. There were forty of them feathered against the bank, the current dragging them at their painters. By now the first assault wave of the King's should have been embarked and crossing the river. I found the Hampshire officer and told him that the battalions had gone the wrong way.

'God Almighty!' he said, and looked sourly down at the river. It was only about twenty yards wide, but the current was strong. He shook his head.

'These bloody boats will be unmanageable in this.'

Ten minutes or so later our guns fell silent: the barrage was over, and looking back we saw the leading files of the King's coming through the gloom. They were to pay a terrible price for their tardiness, but perhaps it would have been the same anyway. I don't really know. For forty minutes the enemy had been pounded mercilessly by one of the most concentrated artillery barrages in history, but our shells had fallen on positions which had been prepared for months. Every German was dug in well below ground and their gun emplacements were strongly protected. Now the Krauts would be standing-to, and already their flares, shining eerily through the mist, began to light up the night sky. Every yard of this river and of the lane behind us was registered by their gunners; every machine-gun traverse had been rehearsed. Now they were going to take their revenge, and I shivered in the cool night air. As the weapon-laden infantry clambered down into their frail craft, it began.

I have no coherent recollection of the next few hours. I think that at the receiving end of a major bombardment one's brain is temporarily numbed by the incessant ear-splitting, shattering, discordant noise. Suddenly my world has shrunk to a few square yards peopled by fleeting images and half-remembered intentions. There is no past and no future, only the present. Someone shouts at me and I shout back. Faces come and go, some familiar and some of strangers; some are curiously devoid of all expression, others are angry and a few have staring terrified eyes. What am I supposed to be doing? I remember, and instinctively I do it. A man drops beside me. He is dead and forgotten in a split second of time. We have no business with the dead; he is nothing.

'Well done, George. Get that man away; get him back to the jeeps. My brain is beginning to work again. The noise fades into the background; it is just a never-ending part of this infernal day. I can think again. How are we doing? Oh my God! Look at that river. I must get to the lane and see what's happening back there. That bloody jeep driver's going too fast: wave him down. The command post is somewhere about here: they'll know something. What's the matter with it? Oh Christ! they're all dead.'

As the hours passed night gave way to day, confusion to understanding, hopes and plans to bitter reality. Information began to reach us. Some of the King's, and later some of A Company the Somersets, had got across the river but the carnage was appalling. The enemy poured machine-gun and mortar fire on to both banks of the river, and bombs were falling into the blood-stained stream itself. The lane running parallel to the river on our side came under intense artillery and mortar fire. Within very few hours all the boats had been destroyed or washed away, spilling their heavily laden occupants into the water to die of their wounds or to drown, and all communication with those across the river was lost. The R/T sets were smashed or in the water and the signallers were dead. Neither regimental aid post had crossed the river and Lieutenant Moore, the King's Medical Officer, was severely wounded in the head. At the left-hand crossing Sergeant George Brown, one of our NCOs who had been awarded the Military Medal a few months before, was standing on the river bank and calmly directing the work of his stretcher-bearers. He was cut down by machine-gun fire and died instantly. At the right-hand crossing Sergeant White, a shy gentle man, was blinded by a shell fragment. Our other NCOs were in the thick of the fury. Sergeant McKay was awarded the DCM and Lance-Corporal Jack Logue the MM for their bravery that day. Jack, a tall gangling Glaswegian, was acting as my runner and he was one of the few men I have ever met who seemed to know no fear.

If the river bank was dreadful, the shell-torn lane — now crowded with troops and the jeeps evacuating the wounded — was not much better. Somehow, with great courage, the stretcher-bearers and the jeep drivers did their work and although I can find no official casualty figures I remember that they evacuated over 400 wounded from the area. A dozen of our little band were killed or wounded. An advanced brigade command post had been established in a dugout near the river. It sustained a direct hit and the three officers inside were killed. As the day wore on morale began to suffer from the incessant punishment. Remnants of the battalions were reorganized and withdrawn, and some troops filtered back into the hills without orders. There was indeed little point in their remaining, because there was no way of crossing the river.

By late afternoon the Brigade Commander was standing with a few officers, myself among them, surveying an almost deserted scene. No bugles sang truce, but the enemy fire had abated for want of targets and a swirling mist drifted over the valley. Behind us in the hills the weary could sleep, but across the river there would be no rest and the wounded would be dying. I made my way back to the advanced dressing station and stretched out on my bedroll. I was too tired to take my boots off and I had an overwhelming sense of disaster. All communication with the men across the river had been lost, but Brigade HQ estimated that about 250 had crossed. It was impossible to guess at the number who had survived, but it was known that the commanding officers of both battalions were lying severely wounded in the bridgehead.

The following day, on the morning of the 13th, a soldier arrived at the A.D.S. He had swum the river from the far bank and carried a message that thirty or forty wounded were lying untreated in the bridgehead. Volunteers were required to swim the river and render first aid. I remembered the old army dictum: 'Don't volunteer for nothing; don't refuse nothing,' and I felt this was an offer I couldn't refuse. There was one slight problem: I am a very poor swimmer and I knew only too well the strength of the current. It was not a problem for long, because the Reverend R. Edwards, Chaplain to the 2nd/4th Hampshires, immediately offered to come with me and tow me across the river. He seemed to have two excellent qualifications for the job: he was a powerful swimmer and his calling should give him a bit of a pull with the Almighty. I was told by Brigade HQ to inform the senior officer in the bridgehead that the Hampshires were going to use a Bailey bridge which 10 Infantry Brigade, on our right, had managed to get across the river and that they would soon be coming to the aid of his beleaguered command.

We went down to the river with a supply of splints, field dressings and morphine: rather a strange reconnaissance party, a parson and a doctor. My commanding officer, Lieutenant-Colonel A.J. Pitkeathly, came with us and was determined to re-establish the ferry by some means or another. Edwards and I tied ourselves together with a length of signal cable and we crabbed our way across, Edwards swimming strongly against the current while I drifted downstream and contributed my usual frog-like breast stroke. Our progress was watched apathetically by a few soldiers sheltering under the steep bank on the far side. They were evidently exhausted by their ordeal and seemed to have lost interest in events. Almost as soon as we climbed up and over the bank I saw the C.O. of the Somersets, Lieutenant-Colonel J.R.I. Platt. He was badly wounded in both legs, and his batman had built a pathetic little sangar of stones and earth around him. That little collection of stones, assembled at goodness knows what risk, may well have saved Platt's life. He had been lying there all night and most of the previous day, but he was quite calm and gave me a sardonic grin as if to say, 'You took your time, chum'. He told me that the others were a few yards ahead, and I found them in a trench a little over three feet deep and half-filled with filthy water. I don't know whether this ditch was an irrigation channel or some remnant of the German defences, but without it there would have been no survivors. The officer in command was a major who greeted me as if I were a visitor to his Mess and asked me to see his colonel, the C.O. of the King's. This poor man, Lieutenant-Colonel J.A. Garnons-Williams, was slumped down in the bottom of the ditch with the water almost as high as his chest. He was in a very bad way and groaning quietly. I never found out where he was hit. The surroundings were hardly conducive to clinical examination and no sooner had I given him an injection of morphine than the most frightful bombardment began. It went on for three or four minutes and I had never experienced anything quite like it. The man to my right, a company sergeant-major, flung himself down in the water and I fell on top of him with my face pressed between his buttocks. He had been in that ditch for thirty-six hours and he had defaecated in his trousers. I would have given a month's pay to get my nose out of the stench but we were all frozen into immobility by the sheer weight of the bombardment. The shells were British and were falling short. The Royal Artillery had for some time used their improved radio communications to evolve a system whereby a large number of guns could be brought to bear at very short notice on relatively small targets. Pin-point accuracy was sacrificed to the destructive and demoralizing impact of a saturating downpour of shells. We were probably the startled recipients of a divisional shoot — I think they called it an Uncle Target — and thanks to our ditch we came to no harm, but it was very bad for the nerves

This cannonade was obviously a prelude to some new action, and when it was over we peered out of the ditch to see what was going on. German soldiers were running towards us and the men around me raised their weapons and began to take aim. Then all along the trench there was a great yell of triumph. The Krauts' hands were in the air: they were surrendering! We stood up, and to our right there was a magnificent sight. The Hampshires were sweeping across the shell-torn ground, bayonets fixed and coming quickly, some towards us but mostly towards the German lines. I had completely forgotten about the Hampshires and the message which I had been told to deliver, and I turned to the colonel. He was unconscious and a few hours later he died, without knowing that he had won.

The Germans were now a few yards away and for some extraordinary reason they were laughing. The grins were wiped off their faces when some of our men began to throw clods of earth at them, but this unsporting behaviour was instantly quelled by the major.* What a magnificent man he was. He had been in that filthy ditch for thirty-six hours with practically nothing to eat or drink and under constant machine-gun, shell and mortar fire. Now he

---

* As we were only on loan to 28 Brigade we did not know the battalion officers by sight, but reading from the King's War Diary I think that this officer was Major Tuohy, O.C. C Company.

leapt out of the trench, shouted 'Come on!' and set off towards the German lines. His men clambered out and stumbled after him, and for the first time I saw the remnant of the two battalions who had forced that terrible crossing. There cannot have been more than forty of them, forty brave men who must have been pushed towards the limit of human endurance and now, filthy and cramped from their ordeal in the ditch, they were limping and staggering in pursuit of an equally brave but beaten enemy. I stood for a minute and watched them go, then there was a cry of 'Stretcher-bearer' and I turned back to my own job. There was an explosion behind me; some German gunner had loosed off a final round and I felt a violent blow in the small of my back. I let out an involuntary yell and then sheepishly realized that the blow was only from a lump of earth flung up by the burst.

Behind us Colonel Pitkeathly and some of our chaps had succeeded in re-establishing the ferry. First they had loaded a new assault boat on to a jeep and Nobby Clarke, the Transport Officer, and an RASC driver tried to get it down to the river. The attempt had to be abandoned because the jeep was machine-gunned and the boat holed in several places. Then someone spotted a boat still afloat and wedged against the bank some distance away, and the indefatigable Padre Edwards swam out and towed it back. As the enemy fire died down another new assault boat was obtained and the German prisoners helped to carry the wounded and man the two-boat ferry.

For a few minutes I was alone. I had left my beret and battledress blouse on the other bank and wore only a shirt and trousers: they were still wet and my boots were caked with stinking mud. The wounded had gone and I looked around at the desolate scene. The bodies of the men who had died lay all about. There was something familiar about that one a few yards away. His body was misshapen and unrecognizable, but his face? Surely I had seen that face before. I went over to where he lay and peered down at him. It was the blond boy from the hills, the boy in the bivouac tent. He would never use his polished bayonet, but in soldier's terms he had done well. He had crossed the river in the teeth of that murderous fire. He must have been among the bravest of the brave, but his mother and his father would never know. His memory would be enshrined only by the ubiquitous epitaph 'Killed in Action'.

Sadly I picked my way through the miserable detritus of battle to where I could see a group of officers and men of the Hampshires. They were standing round their C.O., a fierce-looking little man sitting on an ammunition box. The fierce expression had its origins in piercing blue eyes and a bristling waxed moustache, and a monocle dangled from a thin black ribbon round his neck. He eyed me with disfavour and I remembered that I was far from properly dressed with no badges of either rank or service. I introduced myself and he gave me another item of bad news: their Medical Officer had just had a foot blown off by a 'Schu' mine. It seemed that the catalogue of misfortune would never end and I moved away to leave the Colonel with his acolytes. A despatch rider, dismounted but wearing his helmet, was walking over with a message when there was the unmistakable sound of a stray shell about to descend in our vicinity. The despatch rider flung himself to the ground and slithered almost to the feet of his C.O. The Colonel looked down at him severely, screwed his monocle into his eye, gestured with his hand and said, 'Get up, boy, get up'.

So ended the crossing of the Rapido by 28 Infantry Brigade. For a while we neither knew, nor for that matter much cared, about the fortunes of those on either side of us. We had no hint of the indescribable sufferings of the Poles on Monte Cassino itself. We knew only that we had won and that Cassino had fallen at last. The next few days are a confused blur in my mind. Thousands of men and vehicles poured across the river and into the Liri Valley. The roads and lanes were choked and tempers flared, sometimes in childish idiotic fashion. An infantry colonel who reckoned that my jeep was getting in the way of his jeep shouted, 'Consider yourself under arrest,' and for a daft remark I reckoned that took the biscuit. I gave him what I hoped was a sweet sad smile. One night our trucks were bumping over what we took to be sandbags but they turned out to be the bodies of German soldiers.

The remnants of the brigade had sporadic encounters with the German rearguard — skilful as always, even in defeat. For our part we tried desperately to establish a cohesive line of medical evacuation in the midst of the prevailing chaos and to a large extent we succeeded. This went on for about a week and then the brigade was withdrawn from the pursuit. The fighting men went into some rest area to lick their wounds and we never met up with them again, but because we had been 'on loan' we were given a prize: we were rewarded for our extra-curricular overtime by a totally unexpected and almost unbelievable bounty — a week's leave in Positano.

Half way between Naples and Salerno a finger of land points out into the Tyrrhenian Sea and almost touches the Isle of Capri. Sorrento is on the north of the peninsula, Amalfi and Positano on the south — evocative names which conjure up blissful images of holiday idylls. No place, surely, for war in Positano. Nor was there: it was an unspoiled little seaside resort and was to us a pretty fair imitation of heaven. We camped just outside the town, swam in the sea and sunbathed, and strolled contentedly about the little streets. The few who had some Italian chatted up the locals, and we looked enviously at the boats nodding sleepily in the little harbour. There were no restaurants, for the Italians were desperately short of food, but a few bars were still open and it was these bars that were my undoing — mine and Ken Sharp's.

Ken was our Dental Officer and one of my two best friends. He was a tremendous character, rebellious by nature and with no great regard for the niceties of dress and protocol. A keen debater, he was politically well to the left of centre, and his off-beat views on almost any subject made him a great companion. Very good dentist though he was, his professional duties left him plenty of time to join in any other excitement that was going — the more outrageous the better. He was a staunch friend, utterly reliable and resourceful in time of trouble, and he came to my aid more times than I can remember. If he had a fault it was his inability to remain entirely peaceful when he'd had a few drinks. Alcohol coursed through his veins with alarming rapidity and with unpredictable consequences for those around him. His apparent difficulty at these times in distinguishing friend from foe was a great embarrassment to him, and he was always full of apologies on the morning after, to anyone he happened to have clobbered the night before. One evening when we were making the round of the Positano bars and had swallowed far more Asti Spumante than was good for either of us, we fell to discussing crime, in particular the crime of burglary. It occurred to us that as we had no practical experience of housebreaking, our debate was becoming increasingly sterile. I can't remember which of us was the first to propose that the remedy for this gap in our knowledge was to hand, but the motion was carried unanimously and we staggered out into the street to find a suitable dwelling which we might, in America parlance, burglarize.

It was perhaps unfortunate that we chose a house which involved, for our nefarious purpose, scaling a high stone wall to an upstairs window. Neither of us had the agility of a Raffles even when sober and it is to our credit that we managed the ascent, prised open the window, and tumbled noisily into the house. We groped our way around in the dark, laughing uproariously, until we found ourselves in a bedroom with a terrified Italian lying under a mosquito net. I cannot imagine what the poor man thought when he woke up to find two very drunk British officers leering down at him, but some sense of shame must have overtaken us for we closed his door quietly and wobbled back to the window. It was a bit of a job getting out, but I negotiated the descent safely and began weaving my way back to camp. After fifty yards or so I realized that Ken wasn't with me and sat down on a little wall to await his arrival. He duly appeared out of the gloom, crawling on his hands and knees. I couldn't help thinking that it was a curious way to carry on, but Ken had his own set of rules and if he wanted to crawl home that was his own affair. At this stage of the game I had no intention of starting an argument and he seemed unusually disinclined for conversation. We got back to camp in the end and exchanged a few dignified pleasantries with the guard before falling into bed.

In the morning Ken's curious behaviour was explained. He'd fallen out of the window and broken his ankle. He spent the next six weeks hobbling round in a plaster cast, and the escapade must have taught us a lesson for neither of us has ever committed a burglary since.

PART THREE

REFLECTIONS

On courage, which all of us might need one day; and on job satisfaction, which is arguably the most important thing in life.

The Physiology of Courage

'Courage is the thing. All goes if courage goes.'

Plato was less emphatic than Barrie. He rated Courage as but one of the four cardinal virtues, and found Wisdom, Temperance and Justice to be equally commendable. He used the word temperance to imply moderation and prudence, rather than in the narrow context of abstinence from alcoholic excess, but even so I would cast my vote for Barrie, believing that courage is by far the most attractive quality to which man is heir. I think there is some courage in all of us and would never under any circumstance call a man a coward, for there is no one born who has not been afraid. Indeed it is said that courage is simply the ability to hide one's fear, but I am sure the matter is more complex than that. Lord Moran based his book *The Anatomy of Courage* on his experience as a battalion medical officer in the First World War. He likened each man's store of courage to a bank deposit. Some had more than others, but the amount was finite and the total was depleted by each withdrawal. If too many demands were made, a time would come when there was nothing left. I would go along with that, and for the same reason. It seemed to me, too, that an infantryman's courage gradually ebbed away if he were exposed again and again to the ordeal of battle, and yet survived to fight another, and another, day.

Individual acts of bravery can depend upon a split second of decision, and the margin between hero and coward may have no more reason than the toss of a coin. Years ago I felt desperately sorry for a man who was publicly branded by a Coroner as a coward. He had failed to jump into a canal to rescue a drowning child. He was a non-swimmer, and he reflected just long enough to recoil from what he may have thought was certain death. If only he had jumped. The canal was barely four feet deep and he would have been lauded as a minor hero. He who hesitates may throw his reputation away, and the pity of it is that once the bubble has burst it is gone forever. Ignorance was that man's downfall; he didn't know the canal was shallow and he didn't know how to swim. Had he been better equipped on either count there would have been no problem, and no disgrace.

Knowledge and skill are indeed closely related to the appearance of courage. Fear of the water, or of riding, flying or climbing is steadily reduced as the requisite skills are acquired. Nevertheless, many occupations and sports are inherently dangerous and no amount of skill is an absolute insurance against disaster. Miners, steeplejacks, sailors, jump jockeys, mountain climbers, racing drivers and the like, all know that death is waiting in the wings — but it is this very knowledge, this conscious challenge, that makes the job or sport worthwhile. Who on earth would want to climb a mountain if there were no danger? As far as I am concerned, who on earth would want to climb a mountain anyway?

There must be some relationship between courage and fear, but it is difficult to define — especially in regard to the 'phobias', the quite irrational dread of some circumstance which is not really dangerous at all. I am literally terrified of heights. I *know* that it is not dangerous to climb roof-high on a ladder or to be hauled up to the top of a sailboat's mast, but when I'm up there I cannot relax and am unable properly to control my movements. I cannot bear to see anyone else walk near the edge of a cliff, or even to watch it on film. I cannot be shamed into behaving sensibly, and I must be the only person who has ever crawled on his hands and knees round the top of the Arc de Triomphe in Paris. My wife, on the other hand, has no fear of heights, and I sometimes have to lie on the grass and cover my eyes while she wanders about on the edge of a sheer drop. She cannot understand my unreasonable and unreasoning terror, but she suffers from quite severe claustrophobia and fights for breath if she is in an underground train which has had to stop in a tunnel. Both of us can find an explanation of these absurd phobias in our childhood, and there may be a moral in the telling. Thea, by all accounts a rather naughty child, was often punished by being shut up in a cupboard; and when I was about five years old my two brothers took me by the hands and swung me over a cliff top near Lloyd George's favourite holiday resort, the little Welsh town of Criccieth. I can still hear their uproarious laughter and my screams as I dangled over the sea and rocks below. I have an agarophobic friend who will not leave her home to do the shopping, and others who turn pale if a cat comes into the room. Absurd to us perhaps, but not to them.

Some time ago our son wrote to us from Pakistan. He had just emerged from Afghanistan, where he had accompanied a band of Mujahideen into an encounter with government forces in the bazaar of Russian-occupied Kandahar. His adventures on that and many other occasions are his story, not mine, but he made a comment in his letter which illustrates yet another facet of this complex matter. He wrote:

'It has been said, with great insight, that what keeps a soldier going in the last extremity is the fear, not of death, but of the good opinion of his comrades.'

This is very true. Both fear and the apparent lack of it are contagious, and there are innumerable recorded examples of this contagion both in peacetime and in war.

One night in the Apennines I discovered the terror which solitude can bring to danger, even if that danger is not very great. At the time it was part of my job to spend many hours wandering alone in the mountains, keeping in touch with the various detachments of my unit. It was all quiet on this particular front and I hadn't thought it necessary to tell anyone where I was going. 'All quiet' is a hallowed and rather misleading term meaning that neither side was showing any signs of being unduly offensive, but it was not quiet: the staccato music of war was all around – a familiar almost homely sound as the gunners of both sides earned their pay by laying down harassing fire on a pattern of pre-determined targets. This music has a strange attraction and if I had to be away from my unit for one reason or another I was always glad when I began to hear the sound of our guns on the way back. That sound was home: that was where my friends were. This uncharitable lack of concern for the chaps at the receiving end of our 25-pounders probably indicates a defect in my character – and incoming shells were a different matter altogether. On this particular night, for no reason at all — because I was walking up a track in the middle of nowhere — my little bit of *lebensraum* became a target. I don't think the Kraut gunlayer bore me a personal grudge: he just got it wrong. It was pitch dark, but I saw only one shellburst. From then on my face was buried in the ground with my hands clasped over my head. The noise, magnified by the echoes from the surrounding hills, was quite something. I was lying flatter than flat and the risk of a direct hit was probably remote, but I literally wept with fear. It was soon over and I got up and dusted myself off. I was glad, then, that there had been no witnesses but a few minutes earlier a companion or two, a trouble shared, would have made all the difference.

If solitude and loneliness add an extra dimension to danger, and I'm pretty sure they do, then we must acclaim as something special those remarkable men and women who sail alone across the great oceans and circumnavigate the world in their tiny craft.

I doubt that courage is a constant, specific, immutable attribute which some individuals have, and others have not, and it seems to me that it is a quality which may emerge, or be suppressed, according to the circumstances. It may be fleeting, and one must snatch at it if it is not to pass one by. It cannot simply be defined as the conquest of fear, because I am sure that many individual acts of bravery and many hazardous occupations are carried out by people who are fairly insensitive to that particular danger or are so confident of their own skill, or so hyped up by adrenalin, that they reject the inherent hazard.

This variability in behaviour patterns has attracted the attention of psychiatrists, in the same way that another variable, human intelligence, has bugged them for years. This is a pity, because psychiatrists are trained to be experts in the diagnosis, and sometimes in the treatment, of mental disorders. They have no special expertise in the mental processes of normal people and it is a great mistake to believe that they have. If this fairly obvious fact were more widely appreciated we would not be plagued by these infernal so-called intelligence tests, which seem to be almost as idiotic as the people who invent them. The war in Italy was put at risk because psychiatrists were invited to address themselves to the problem of fear. It was not called fear at the time — it was called 'exhaustion'. This was a euphemism for the condition which in the First World War was called shell-shock. The psychiatrists, knowing absolutely nothing of war, soldiers, shell-shock, exhaustion or any other relevant matter, decided to set up a number of rehabilitation centres where 'exhausted' soldiers could be sedated and given rest and good food until such time as they felt keen on going back to get themselves killed. News of these rehabilitation centres spread like wildfire, and the troops became exhausted in droves.

All the aspects of this problem that I have mentioned so far are within the perception of everyone. They are examples of active courage: the commission of some specific act, or deliberate and perhaps habitual exposure to known danger. There is another kind of courage, passive courage, of which I may lay claim to special knowledge by virtue of my calling. To those patients who come under the surgeon's knife and the anaesthetists's mask, the stake is the same as the soldier's – life or death. The odds are better, but the implicit risk is there and is, more often than not, part of a venture into the unknown. I have carried out thousands of operations and it is an astonishing, and to me inexplicable, fact that I have hardly ever seen an adult patient show any overt sign of fear. One task that I always detested was to tell an old man or woman that his or her leg would have to be amputated, sometimes above the knee, because of what must have seemed to the patient a relatively trivial condition, gangrene of the toes. These old people were obviously startled and shocked by my explanations but never once did any of them flinch, or break down, or cry when I told them what needed to be done. The same remarkable courage was shown by every one of the multitude of women whose breasts I have removed for cancer. I expect some of them wept in the privacy of their homes but their stoicism in public was exemplary.

Modern surgical operations are on the whole very successful, and if all goes well they are not particularly distressing. Occasionally, however, all does not go well, and it is when unexpected complications ensue that the patient's fortitude may be tested to the utmost. Two families stand out in my memory and there was a remarkable similarity between them. In each case it was the husband and father who was the patient, and in both the operation was that of partial gastrectomy – removal of most of the stomach for duodenal ulcer. This is an operation I have carried out over twelve hundred times and I was, I think justifiably, rather proud of my technique and results, but these two patients went almost unbelievably wrong. The first was Mr M, a very good-looking quietly spoken Irishman in early middle age. He was also blessed with a lovely wife and daughter. I told him that he needed an operation for his ulcer and he enquired in his soft Irish brogue:

'Would that be the operation called partial gastrectomy?'

'That's right.'

'Both my brothers had that operation,' he went on.

'That's good,' I said cheerfully, 'so you'll know all about it.'

There was a little pause and then he said, 'They both died'.

We were standing round his bed in the ward, and there was a shocked silence. I could not think of any adequate response, and in the end I put a hand on his shoulder.

'Don't worry,' I said, 'you won't have any trouble here.'

The operation was completely straightforward and uneventful but after about a week there was the first sign of trouble. For no apparent reason he began to vomit, and two days later I re-opened his abdomen to find that the remnant of stomach left behind had been drawn up and welded to the diaphragm by an adhesion nearly an inch thick. I had never seen this complication before nor have I seen it since, nor has it to my knowledge ever been described, nor do I know any other surgeon who has seen it. Cutting the adhesion away to free the stomach remnant took only a few minutes. He recovered rapidly from the operation and I went on a pre-arranged holiday to the south of France. When I returned he was again very ill. He had developed a large abscess under the diaphragm, and one of my colleagues had operated on him yet again and had drained the abscess by two tubes, one to the right of the abdomen and the other to the left. This operation undoubtedly saved his life, but within a peculiarly short time the right hand tube had eroded into his small gut and the left hand tube into his large gut. Faeces were pouring from one side of his abdomen and irritating intestinal juice from the other. I tried to wipe the look of horror from my face but his only comment, a characteristic one, was to ask if I'd had a good holiday. Never once did this man, his lovely wife, or his gorgeous daughter complain of these repeated disasters or of his suffering. Gradually his wounds healed and after many weeks he was completely cured, save in one respect: he had developed a large incisional hernia where the weakened and infected scars had given way. It was an ugly bulge and I explained rather hesitantly that he had a choice: I could repair the hernia by a fourth operation, or he could wear a permanent belt. We grinned at each other and he said quietly, 'I think I'll take the belt.'

In later years I wondered if there were some genetic defect in the healing process which affected these three brothers. Why on earth should they all have had such disastrous consequences from a straightforward routine procedure? The basic trouble must have been seepage from internal stitching of a type which is normally very secure. Why did the tubes erode so rapidly into the gut on both sides? We shall never know.

Mr R. was if anything even more disastrous, but there was a great deal of similarity between the two families. He was older than Mr M. but his wife was equally devoted and charming, and he too had a lovely grown-up daughter. The initial operation was rather more difficult than Mr M.'s and the ulcer was very extensive. It had a peculiar feature which I had not seen before and which would not, I think, be intelligible to the lay reader; but I had a premonition of possible trouble. After a few days it was clear that further surgery would be required and I re-opened his abdomen, but without any great apprehension. However, the operation proved appallingly difficult. The tissues were densely matted, swollen and distorted, and after nearly two hours I had failed to locate and define the trouble. A colleague, one of my oldest friends and a very skilled surgeon, happened to look in to the operating theatre and I asked him, in some despair, to scrub up and help me. I always remember his comment after he had dissected patiently for some time. 'I feel,' he said, 'as though I am wandering in a strange garden.' We worked on for another hour, and eventually were able to find our way through this 'strange garden' and display the source of the trouble. Together we devised and carried out an operation which had never been done before, but which met the unique circumstances of the case and which offered a hope of recovery, provided the stitches held in the sodden and infected tissues.

They, the stitches, did not hold; and from the fourth

postoperative day there was an appalling and increasing discharge of highly corrosive duodenal juices. Such a discharge has the effect of causing a gross disturbance of the patient's blood, upsetting the proportions of the various salts and proteins which are essential to life and which must be replaced, together with the fluid lost, by intravenous infusion. The calculation of the correct amounts of the essential constituents is based on daily laboratory tests, but it was exceedingly difficult in Mr R's case to keep pace with the enormous fluid and salt loss. He became more gravely ill with each succeeding day, the skin of his abdomen was burned and excoriated by the corrosive digestive juices, and he was plagued by interminable needle punctures either to take blood samples or to maintain the massive intravenous infusions. His legs became swollen and his general state pitiable. We did our best to explain what was going on, but it is difficult to explain disaster, and his suffering was plain for all to see. He could not have been blamed if he had cursed the lot of us, and me in particular, but he never did. Neither he, nor his wife or daughter, ever uttered a word of complaint.

The dedication and skill of the resident doctors and nursing staff, and the devotion of his family kept him alive, and after many weeks he made a full and almost miraculous recovery. One of the nurses, who was a novitiate nun, prayed for him several times a day and in a weak moment, for I am an atheist, I told my wife that if he recovered I too would give thanks to God. She kept me to my promise and I duly said my little piece in the church of Thomas à Becket at Pagham in Sussex. Perhaps the nurse's prayers did get an answer, but scientifically speaking it was a complicated business for the Lord to take on. About a year later I was driving to another hospital and I saw Mr R running along the pavement. It was a very happy moment.

The soldier, the lifeboatman, the mountaineer, the fighter pilot and the other men and women who face continual danger know that they *may* die at any moment. We all know that one day we *will* die, but there are many who are afflicted by terminal disease and know that they are about to die, that their hour has come. I wish I knew more of the state of mind of these people and in the natural course of events I expect that one day I shall. In the main their faces were inscrutable, and I think that many were able to accept, and then dismiss, the knowledge of impending death. As their end drew near it seemed to me that they forbore to ask the question which must have been uppermost in their minds. They did not wish to hear the truth spoken aloud. I can remember only two patients who asked me outright if they were going to die. The first was an old nun with inoperable cancer, a delightful woman whom I used to tease because she was always surreptitiously telling her beads under the bedclothes and losing them in her capacious knickers. When she asked, 'Am I dying?' there was something in her eyes which made dissimulation impossible.

'Yes,' I told her, 'you are.'

She nodded, and dismissed me by picking up her book from the bedside table.

Never in all my years of hospital practice did I see anyone flinch from the inevitable outcome, but sometimes courage flared out like a beacon. One such was the second patient who asked me the direct question. He was a man of ninety-two years of age and came under my care with a strangulated umbilical hernia, a condition which could indeed have been lethal at his age.

'Am I going to die?' he asked.

'No,' I said, 'I don't think so.'

He smiled, showing his few yellowing teeth, and took me by the hand.

'If I do,' he said, 'don't upset yourself, my boy. I've had a good life.'

I wasn't exactly a boy; I was over fifty at the time, but I made damn sure that fine old boy survived.

The friend who helped me in the interminable second operation on Mr R is now dead, and when I read the address at his memorial service I said of him that he had the quality of compassion – the ability to find words of comfort for those who were beyond all else. I always had difficulty in finding those words, especially when fresh words had to be found on each visit to the bedside. I was in late middle age before I discovered that words were not always necessary, and that taking the hand of a dying patient gave a degree of comfort out of all proportion to the simplicity of the gesture. It has something of the merit which a priest may attach to the laying on of hands, and I think it works because it parts the veil of solitude.

The patient feels that he is not alone in his travail, and the physical contact is as welcome to the dying as to a lonely child.

It has been my privilege to witness very many instances of courage, both active and passive. When this courage bears fruit one can rejoice, but when it ends in death there is an infinite sadness and a feeling that with the dead has gone something of the human spirit which is beyond compare.

Job Satisfaction

'I suppose work must be good for you, but there's no money in it.'

My friend Hubert, a stockbroker.

Some time ago a bespectacled young man came to lay a new carpet in our bathroom. I was lost in admiration of his dexterity and speed, and complimented him on his skill while we were drinking the ritual cup of coffee in the kitchen. He accepted my praise and began to reminisce.

'Do you remember your first operation?' he asked. 'I'll never forget my first carpet: it was worth a thousand quid, and I cut it an inch at a time. It took me five hours.'

It had taken him only twenty minutes to cut and lay *our* carpet, but then it wasn't worth a thousand quid. His question had set me thinking. I do remember my first operation, the first that I did entirely on my own without one of my seniors assisting or looking over my shoulder. It was not much of an operation – an appendix, in the middle of the night, in a big hospital for sick children but for the first time I felt, however mistakenly, that I had a life in my hands. The feeling is difficult to recapture. It was certainly not one of power or self-importance because I was all too painfully aware of my inexperience and limitations, and of worry that the diagnosis might turn out to be wrong. It was a frightening, lonely feeling. Perhaps it could be likened to the first time a single-handed sailor turns his craft towards the open sea and leaves the land behind. Frightening, exciting and rewarding. Probably much the same as cutting your first carpet.

I thought of other operations too. How many of them can I remember, and why? This faculty of recall was discussed a while ago on the television programme *Question Time*, and I was rather taken with a query which someone put to the panel:

'What in your life would you most like forgotten, and what would you most like to be remembered?'

The members of the panel were perhaps a little embarrassed and they chose to treat the question lightly, but had it been a private discussion their answers might have been more revealing and they would have agreed, I think, that the first part of the question posed an inescapable paradox. It is not possible to forget what you would most like to forget, and if other people were involved they will not forget it either. Like any other surgeon I have performed a good many thousand operations and by the very nature of things the vast majority were successful, or if there were mistakes they were trivial and reparable, or if the operation failed in the end it was because the disease was inherently incurable. Most of these I have forgotten completely, but there were a few when the patient died because of me — never, I hope, because of negligence but from errors of judgement. These I would give anything to forget, but I cannot: every detail remains with me still. The old jibe that a surgeon buries his mistakes is very far from the truth.

Surgeons remember a particular operation or group of operations, either for technical considerations or because of the personality of an individual, or for a combination of both reasons. Some procedures are eminently forgettable, and in common with most of my colleagues I detested operating on varicose veins; nor can I pretend that I went a bundle on that rather unromantic condition which laymen call haemorrhoids and doctors call piles.

Then there is a large group of straightforward run of the mill operations any one of which can be recalled only by a quirk of behaviour or circumstance, or occasionally by some freakish complication. In this category are appendicectomy, hernial repair, removal of the gall-bladder, operations on the kidney, bladder and prostate, gastrectomy, and a host of other routine procedures. They are effective and satisfying, but they do not linger in the memory.

Most surgeons have a special interest in some aspect of their work, and mine was in two operations which are traditionally associated with the loss of a considerable amount of blood — removal of the thyroid gland and removal of the breast. My anaesthetists and I collaborated in devising techniques which reduced the blood loss almost to zero, and this lent a touch of elegance to the procedures — which made them enjoyable to us in the way that any craftsmen take pleasure in work of delicacy and precision.

I disliked amputations, and operations for removal of those parts of the bowel which left the patient with an artificial opening, an ileostomy or colostomy. Patients tolerate and manage these overt alterations in their anatomy remarkably well and the procedures are often life-saving, but they are aesthetically distasteful to patient and surgeon alike. However, some of them are far from easy, and surgeons specializing in that line of work derive much satisfaction from the exquisite skill which they bring to bear on the problem.

Emergency abdominal surgery is particularly gratifying. The operations are often required in the long watches of the night; they are usually easy, life-saving and totally successful. At times, driving home in the early morning after repairing a perforated duodenal ulcer, operating on a strangulated hernia, relieving an obstruction of the bowel or removing a ruptured spleen, I have felt myself to be one of an elite, to be set a little apart from those other chaps on the road, driving who knows where in the dawn. Such delusions of grandeur can, alas, be short-lived because even in emergency surgery we do not always win. In this field, a massive internal abdominal haemorrhage is a dramatic event and is usually due to either a ruptured spleen or to a so-called ruptured ectopic gestation — which means that a pregnancy has developed in the fallopian tube instead of its proper place, the womb. The operative treatment of both these conditions is simple, but once, when operating on a youngish woman who was thought to have a 'ruptured ectopic' I found that the diagnosis was wrong: the belly was full of blood but it seemed to be coming from higher up the abdomen. Surgeons are very familiar with haemorrhage, and provided we have the necessary help and equipment we are not unduly alarmed. There is something a little menacing about the quiet hiss of a severed artery in the depths of a wound, and severe venous bleeding can be genuinely intimidating, but there are well-established procedures for dealing with almost any situation and usually the surgeon takes the opportunity of giving a little demonstration to his juniors. It is a chance to show off some of the tricks of the trade. That night my inbuilt confidence soon evaporated: the bleeding was torrential but I couldn't find its source. I was hampered by the presence of the omentum, a fatty apron which we call 'the abdominal policeman' because it wraps itself around any focus of trouble within the abdomen. Ninety-nine times out of a hundred this protective embrace is to the patient's advantage but in this instance it was a damned nuisance. One could liken the problem to that of finding a leak in the hold of a ship when the hold was full of water and a cargo of cotton. The closer I got to the source of the trouble the more unmanageable it became. I was quite unable to control it, and my assistants poured twenty bottles of blood into the unfortunate woman's veins while I struggled in vain to staunch the flow. She died on the operating table – with thirty pints of blood, ten of hers and twenty of ours, on the floor or in saturated swabs hung up by the dozen in the operating theatre. It was a ghastly and unforgettable sight, and when it was over I sat in the surgeons' room with my head in my hands, feeling sick and humiliated.

The mystery remained unsolved until the autopsy the following day, when all the interested parties assembled in the postmortem room. Few of my readers will have been in a postmortem room and I cannot recommend a visit, even as spectator. These places have a curious smell: not the awful smell of death, of putrefaction, but an odour peculiarly their own – as indefinable but as recognizable to habitués as the smell of a football changing room. The mortuary attendant cultivates a proprietorial air of having seen it all before, of casual familiarity with death and all its appurtenances, but I fancy there is just a touch of bluster behind the outward assurance. A postmortem room would not be the place for an imaginative man to spend the night. As well as the smell there is an ambient chill which the single radiator does little to dispel and which seems in keeping with the cold marble slab, the buckets and the hose. The architect of an autopsy room has an unenviable task: he has to cater for two categories of occupant – the quick and the dead. A measure of refrigeration is deemed appropriate for the latter and, by and large, the living are left to get on as best they can. At one hospital where I worked the senior pathologist, a professor, had a rare and, to my mind, very sensible regard for his comfort and that of his fellow workers. He insisted on a roaring coal fire on all but the hottest days, and it was quite remarkable how this transformed the atmosphere of what is, of necessity, a rather forbidding establishment. I sometimes feel that my professor's philosophy could do something for the shrinking congregations in our churches. Imagine how much more acceptable would be a sermon with the celebrant's face illumined and his words punctuated by the dancing flames and lively crackle of great logs burning in a noble fireplace. I commend this thought to the Archbishop of Canterbury, or indeed, to any sectarian rival who may see some merit in the notion.

I must apologize for this aside, this digression from what was, and is, a grim business. It is in the postmortem room that the presiding genius, the pathologist, pronounces upon the diagnosis of his clinical colleagues; upon accidents, suicides and now and then, a murder. It is in this room that the truth will out. Not that the truth is written on a piece of paper for all to see: it is here that the skill and experience of the pathologist comes into its own. He must dissect, and peer, and take away and examine under a microscope, and analyse and ponder and deduce — and then decide, for he is the final arbiter. He has all the time in the world and his work is not constrained within the bounds of a limited incision nor hampered by the flux of blood. He can do what damage is necessary to get at the truth because life is no longer of any moment. All his customers are already dead: the truth is all that matters. Why did the patient die? On his answer, and none will gainsay him, may depend a reputation, a fortune, a lifetime in prison. No wonder they are thoughtful, serious-minded men.

My poor little lady, so diminished now, was wheeled in and lifted on to the slab, her head pillowed on a rough-shaped block of wood. The stitched wound on her abdomen bore witness to my futile struggle of the night before. The pathologist, my friend of many years, took up his knife and on the other side of the slab I edged closer. Soon I would know why she had died and I had failed. What the hell could it have been? God! What a mess. I will draw a veil over the next half-hour. This sort of thing is neither pleasant to watch nor to read about, but at the end there is the truth.

She had an aneurysm (a balloon-like swelling) of her splenic artery, the main artery to the spleen. It was the size of a large grape and had eroded and fashioned for itself a nest in the pancreas (what a butcher could call the sweetbread). The omentum, the abdominal policeman, had sensed trouble ahead and had gone to the rescue, wrapping itself around and sticking on to everything in the vicinity. So far, so good, but then disaster had struck; the aneurysm had burst, letting her blood pour out under pressure to tear a great hole in the pancreas and then find the paths of least resistance into the tangled web of omentum, tearing that and then freely into the abdominal cavity and past my packs to spill on to the operating table and then the floor: thirty pints of it. Now I knew the truth, and I was left to wonder if a better surgeon than I could have stemmed that awful torrent.

Such aneurysms of the splenic artery are rare, and ruptured aneurysms even more so, but a few months after this disaster I operated on another − but what a different story it turned out to be. This time the aneurysm, a huge one, had adhered to the wall of the stomach and had burst into it so that the leakage of blood, massive as it was, poured into the stomach itself and not freely into the abdominal cavity. This meant that I could see quite easily what needed to be done and it was a simple matter to tie the splenic artery, remove the aneurysm and spleen, and repair the hole in the stomach. The patient went home, completely cured, in a fortnight, but he suffered a mild attack of pleurisy while he was in the hospital and was extremely ungracious about it. He was rather a disagreeable man and it was just the sort of thing, he implied, that one could expect from the National Health Service. I was very tempted to tell him how lucky he had been, and that if his aneurysm hadn't stuck to his stomach he might well have been dead.

If both patient and surgeon are to get the maximum satisfaction from an operation, the patient must be permanently cured of symptoms which are causing him or her great distress. It is not enough for a condition to be *potentially* nasty. Many a woman must wonder if removal of her breast for a small painless lump is a fair exchange. *We* know that it is, but *they* may not think so. There are of course many diseases where the optimum criterion of swapping severe illness for total and permanent cure is fulfilled, but I have a particular affection, if that is the right word, for the operative treatment of a certain rather rare condition. I have done the operation only three times, but on each occasion with immense satisfaction. Doctors never use a short word where a long word will do, and the malady rejoices in the name of gastro-jejuno-colic fistula — which is our way of saying that an ulcer has caused a communication between the stomach, the small bowel and the large bowel. This reduces the sufferer to a truly pitiable state with great loss of weight, continuous diarrhoea and foul eructations. Left untreated the patient would die, but he can be completely restored to permanent good health by a painstaking, lengthy and technically very interesting and challenging procedure. One of my three patients, on whom I operated over a quarter of a century ago, still sends me a calendar every Christmas.

However, if I had to give pride of place to any one surgical memory I would award it to a trivial operation many years ago because of its unexpected, startling, almost fairy-tale outcome. The girl, in her early twenties, was not even my patient, but one of my colleagues was unexpectedly called away in the middle of his operating list and he asked me to do the operation for him. I had noticed the girl in the ward: one could not help noticing her because she was fiendishly ugly. I didn't know anything about her history but she must have been one of those people who have a horror of operations, and she had tolerated for years the gradual development of a swelling in the floor of her mouth. It had eventually reached the size of a Jaffa orange, bulging below her chin and forcing her tongue up so that it protruded permanently from her mouth. It was only because she was now unable to eat that she had agreed to have the swelling removed. She looked like a gargoyle and not unnaturally took little pride in her dress or hair. She was, in a word, repulsive.

The swelling turned out to be a simple cyst, and its removal was extremely easy. It shelled out through an incision inside her mouth, like a gigantic pea out of a pod. A few stitches and the operation was over: it took less than a quarter of an hour. When I saw the girl in the ward a couple of days later I could not believe my eyes, and nor could she. She was staring at herself in a hand mirror. She was a beauty! The nurses had risen to the occasion, as they always do. They had shampooed and set her hair and her face was skilfully made up with their own cosmetics. A pretty nightdress had come from somewhere. Overnight, as if a good fairy had touched her with a magic wand, she had been transformed from a gargoyle into a truly lovely girl. She went home the next day, and I don't think that she knew who I was. I never spoke to her, but no operation has ever given me greater pleasure.

Now that I have retired, I have little nostalgia for the practice of surgery. I was glad to give it up for one particular reason – the prevalence of that group of diseases, differing widely in their degree of lethality but all coming under the layman's heading of 'cancer'. Very many patients are cured of cancer by surgery or by other means, but it is common knowledge that many are not. The operations for cancer are often elegant and precise, but it is heartbreaking to carry out such an operation to no avail. Other professions are not subjected to this heartbreak: if one is a builder of bridges and builds them properly, one can be reasonably sure that they won't fall down, but no amount of technical skill can guarantee success in the field of cancer, and so often it seemed to me that those who succumbed were such delightful and courageous people. Their ghosts were always there to haunt me and to point the finger of failure.

Looking back into the shadows, as old people do, I see two bright pinpoints of light – two moments when I came near to total fulfilment, but which have nothing to do with what was supposedly my life's work, moments which many would think trivial but others might recognize for what they were to me.

One was when, for the first time, I won a motor race. The occasion is not difficult to recall because in my short racing career I won only four outright. It was in the Spring of 1963, on Easter Monday, at Brands Hatch. I had started from scratch in a handicap race, and I managed to catch all the other competitors. Handicap races are always exciting, and the huge Easter Monday crowd must have been entertained because they gave me the traditional Brands Hatch ovation: blowing their car horns in a raucous tumult which I could hear above the sound of my engine as I completed my cooling-down lap.

Motor racing has a gladiatorial quality which is rather unattractive, but I found fascinating and compelling the overnight transformation of the venue from grey desolation into a feast of colour, hectic activity, fierce aspiration and determined contention. Even the shadow of death can never dim the brilliance of the scene.

The second moment was even more fleeting and was in, or rather on, a sailboat in Chichester Harbour. I am a poor sailor: I learned too late in life, I have no natural talent and in rough weather I get sick; but on that perfect day I was at the helm of my Condor catamaran, a very fast and graceful boat. The sky was blue, flecked only by wisps of cirrus cloud, and the wind was steady and abeam as we came howling out of Emsworth channel, passing other boats as though they were standing still. My son, whom I love dearly, was stretched out to his full length on the trapeze and as the windward hull lifted and we flashed across the water, we looked at each other and smiled. All our worries dissolved in that instant of total and companionable pleasure.

Epilogue

This book has been largely concerned with the reactions of individuals to pain, distress and fear. My calling has made me something of an expert in such matters, but I have not until now ventured any comment on the strongest and sometimes the most enduring emotion of all − love. Here I have no claim to expertise and I do not know to whom we should turn for counsel: to a woman who has been faithful to one man for the whole of her married life, or to a man who has taken a score of mistresses? Both must know a thing or two, but does either comprehend the whole? Should we turn to the priest, who is ordained to love (with a few sectarian reservations) each and every one of us, yet is denied the fulfilment of a love for just one other? We cannot disregard the imagery of novelists: emotion is their stock-in-trade and they are more astute and articulate observers than the rest of us. They can pick and choose from their experience and that of others to make a composite but believable whole, and sometimes it may seem that love has its purest expression upon the printed page. A writer has the power to embellish life itself and it is sad that many seek only to demean it.

It seems that physical beauty is but a minor ingredient in this strange and powerful alchemy. One cannot stand in a busy street or on a crowded beach without remarking that we humans are in the main, a funny looking lot. Yet love, true love, is all about us... that pimply youth with his arm stretched around the waist of his fat girl friend: perhaps they will marry, and by a coupling too fearsome to contemplate will beget more of the same; and love them too. Not far away there is that ageing vicar, who threw away his reputation and his living for love of a dumpy bespectacled parishioner. Love is surely blind, and for explanation we must turn, as we do so often, to the poet. John Lyly, in the sixteenth century, had the truth of it.

> Cupid and my Campaspe played
> At cards for kisses; Cupid paid:
> He stakes his quiver, bow, and arrows,
> His mother's doves, and team of sparrows;
> Loses them too; then down he throws
> The coral of his lip, the rose
> Growing on's cheek (but none knows how);
> With these, the crystal of his brow,
> And then the dimple of his chin;
> All these did my Campaspe win.
> At last he set her both his eyes —
> She won, and Cupid blind did rise.
> O Love! has she done this to thee?
> What shall, alas! become of me?

So, my story ends as it began; with a sad little tale which some might think unlikely.